LARGE PRINT

HELPFUL HOUSEHOLD HINTS

Publications International, Ltd.

Cover images: Shutterstock.com; Thinkstock

Interior images: Shutterstock.com; Thinkstock; Getty Images

Contributing editor: Lisa Brooks

Louis Weber, CEO
Publications International, Ltd.
73 73 North Cicero Avenue
Lincolnwood, Illinois 60712

ISBN-13: 978-1-4508-8187-6
ISBN-10: 1-4508-8187-4

Manufactured in China.

8 7 6 5 4 3 2 1

CONTENTS

CHAPTER 1
Supplies and Strategies

No one has time to clean anymore. There is too much else to do. But most of us would prefer not to come home to a total disaster area, so cleaning has to be dealt with sooner or later.

The time it takes you to tidy up is time taken away from work and play, and it has got to be time well spent. With the right cleaning strategy, you can keep the drudgery to a minimum and give yourself the maximum amount of valuable living time.

Cleaning is hard work, but with the right tools and cleaning products, a game plan, and the helpful cleaning tips in this book, your cleaning load will be lighter than ever before. You'll enjoy a neat living environment and time to devote to yourself, your family, and your friends.

Hurried does not have to mean helter-skelter. Your cleaning schedule for both regular and seasonal care should be organized in a way that makes you comfortable: You may choose to clean for an hour every morning, two hours after work, or all Saturday morning. As long as you have a schedule that leaves room for spontaneity, you'll stay ahead of housework.

Concentrate on one room at a time; don't run all over your house or apartment pushing dirt around here and there. Stick with one room until it is sparkling clean. You'll have the reward and encouragement of its good looks when you're ready to proceed to the next task.

Basic day-to-day chores, such as beds, dishes, baths, laundry, and floor care, require a firm routine. Big tasks, such as closets, ovens, and silver, are often best tackled on impulse and require an elastic plan. If a big chore is hanging over your head and you keep putting it off,

wait. It will be there when you are up to it, and you'll probably do a better job if you are ready to tackle it. Remember that when you are in the mood to clean, your cleaning tasks will get done much faster if there are no interruptions. So turn on the answering machine and send the kids who are too little to help to visit a friend, and concentrate on the task at hand.

Most big cleaning jobs will go much faster if you have help. Divide the labor among all the members of the household, including the children, or invite a friend to help out. You can reciprocate when his garage needs cleaning.

CLEANING PLAN

Here is a general plan for cleaning a home. We hope you'll use it as a starting point for making your own cleaning strategy.

EVERY DAY

- Remove litter from carpets and hard-surface floors with a vacuum cleaner.

- Wash dishes, and wipe countertops and cooking appliances.

- Empty kitchen garbage containers.

- Wipe basins and bathtubs.

- Make beds and straighten rooms.

AS NEEDED

- Vacuum carpets and hard-surface floors thoroughly.

- Vacuum upholstery and drapes.

- Dust and/or polish furniture.

- Clean the range and wipe out the refrigerator.

- Wash the kitchen and bathroom floors.

- Clean toilets, fixtures, and bathroom mirrors.

- Change bed linens.

- Empty wastepaper baskets.

SEASONAL

- Surface-clean rugs and carpets, using a carpet-cleaning solution or an absorbent powder.

- Remove old wax, apply new wax, and buff hard-surface floors.

- Wash throw rugs.

- Shampoo upholstered furniture.

- Wash lamp shades, walls, and woodwork.

- Dust books, pictures, and lamps.

- Clean mirrors, TVs, picture frames, and art objects.

- Clean ovens, microwave, freezer, refrigerator, and other appliances.

- Wash bathroom carpeting and shower curtain.

- Organize closets.

- Turn mattresses, wash pads and pillow covers, and air or wash pillows.

- Clean screens and wash windows.

YEARLY

- Vacuum rug pads and the backs of rugs.

- Shampoo carpets, clean rugs, and turn rugs to equalize wear.

- Wash curtains, blinds, and shades; Clean draperies.

- Clean closets and cabinets.

- Wash or dry-clean bedspreads, blankets, and slipcovers.

- Clean out the garage, basement, and workshop.

EMERGENCIES

- Remove spots and stains while they are fresh.

DUST OR VACUUM, WHICH TO DO FIRST?

If you have mats at all the entrances to your home, both inside and outside, you'll cut your cleaning time almost in half. Mats also make dusting the first logical step in cleaning, since your floors and carpets will not release clouds of dust as you go about your cleaning tasks.

Anyone who tells you not to dust until you have vacuumed your floors needs a new vacuum cleaner.

A good vacuum cleaner will not spew dust over cleaned surfaces. If your vacuum cleaner releases dust or has a dusty or burning smell when you turn it on, you probably need to replace the bag, empty a bagless vacuum's canister, or clean any filters. If your vacuum uses a disposable dust bag, clean it frequently so that your vacuum will clean with maximum efficiency.

Dusting is more than picking up minute particles of lint or airborne residue on a picture frame. Dusting is scraping dirt and grime off windowsills; vacuuming eraser rubbings and food crumbs; getting all the orange seeds and gum wrappers off the living room furniture; and on and on. If you vacuum the floor first, all the litter you dust off other surfaces can end up on your freshly vacuumed floor.

The best plan is to dust with your vacuum cleaner. Instead of releasing dust and debris into the air and onto other surfaces in the room, start at the ceiling and dust everything from moldings to baseboards with your vacuum cleaner. Your vacuum cleaner will remove dust from hard-to-reach areas, such as the tops of doors and the inside areas of radiators, and do a much more thorough cleaning job than a dust cloth.

CLEAN A ROOM QUICKLY

Before you start to clean a room, face the fact of dirt. Cleaning is dirty work and your clothes will get soiled, so dress the part. Pull on a pair of old jeans, roll up the sleeves on a tattered shirt, and attack the grime with your full attention.

Gather together all the cleaning supplies you will need. Carrying them in a tote basket will save extra steps between your cleaning closet and your work site. Then, take everything out of the room that does not belong in it. Put small decorative items into a basket and out of harm's way, and put the dirty items that you want to clean separately, such as figurines and metal objects that need polishing, in a box or basket and take them to the kitchen. Don't redistribute anything until you have finished cleaning the room.

Pull all the furniture out from the walls. Turn back rugs at the edges, and take up small scatter rugs to make vacuuming the floor easier. Choose a starting point and work your way around the room. The law of gravity applies: Dust settles downward, so avoid dirtying what you have just cleaned.

WHEN COMPANY COMES ON 10-MINUTE NOTICE

The phone rings; it's a friend from school in town for a meeting or one of your mother's cousins who happens to be in the neighborhood. The surprise visitor will be at your door in 10 minutes, and your home must be ready to go on show. The following whirlwind routine will help you present a neat facade:

- Gather everything that is sitting where it doesn't belong in the entry and living areas, and dump it all into an empty laundry basket. Hide the filled basket in a closet.

- Stack newspapers and magazines on the coffee table or floor, and plump the furniture pillows.

- Give the bathroom sink and toilet a once-over, and straighten the rug and towels. Shine the mirror with tissue, and shove scattered items back into the medicine cabinet.

- Rinse the dishes, and stack them neatly in the kitchen sink or put them in the dishwasher. Wipe the countertops.

- Close the doors to rooms you don't want to display.

- Try to relax.

Always work from the top down. Clean floors last.

With the appropriate attachment on your vacuum cleaner, dust moldings, door frames, draperies, lamp shades, blinds, shutters, pictures, wall hangings, mantels, shelves, vents, radiators, and baseboards. Vacuum upholstered furniture, as well as wood, plastic, and chrome furniture. Wipe smudges off doorknobs, light switches, and walls with an all-purpose cleaner.

Hard-surface floors are next. Using the floor-brush attachment on your vacuum cleaner, thoroughly vacuum all hard-surface flooring, such as tile, linoleum, vinyl, and wood. Now straighten the rugs that were folded back for cleaning, and vacuum them slowly. Fluff up the carpet pile.

That's it. Simply replace the furniture, dust your bric-a-brac and replace it, and your room is clean. You don't have to polish the wood furniture, wash the windows, or scrub the floors; save these special tasks for another time. It is more efficient.

TOOLS OF THE TRADE

A well-stocked cleaning center is the hurried housecleaner's best friend. You will be more likely to start your cleaning chores and to finish the task if you have everything you need on hand and in one place. A cleaning closet will save you time and steps; it is the efficient beginning to all the quick and easy cleaning methods in this book. You may not need everything that's listed here, but as you read this section, think about the cleaning tasks you perform regularly and stock your cleaning closet with the tools that will help you accomplish them most efficiently and quickly.

Storing all your cleaning equipment and supplies in one place—your cleaning closet—will save you time and effort every time you clean.

Before you supply your cleaning closet, make sure the closet has a place to store all the cleaning tools and products you buy. If you can't fit them all into one orderly place, you'll waste time digging around under the sink for the cleanser and going out to the garage for your mop. Put up pegboard or

hooks to hang brushes and mops. They'll not only be easier to lay your hands on, but they'll last longer if they are hung. Install plenty of shelves to hold bottles and cartons. This will get dangerous cleaning products out of the reach of children and give you space to store a full battery of cleaning supplies, so that when you find time to clean, everything you need will be handy.

Baskets are used for carrying supplies from one room to another and for collecting dishes you want to take to the kitchen to wash, the collectibles you want to polish, and/or the toys the kids left in the family room.

Brushes are available in a variety of sizes: a hard-bristled scrub brush, toilet brushes (one for each bathroom), a radiator brush, and other soft- and medium-bristled brushes for scrubbing and dusting.

Double compartment buckets hold both your cleaning solution and rinse water.

Chamois are expensive, but they will last almost indefinitely when properly handled. Nothing absorbs water better than soft leather, so your chamois is perfect for drying washed cars and windows. After you use it, wash your chamois in a detergent solution, rinse thoroughly, squeeze out the water, stretch it to full size, and place it on a flat surface to dry. Don't wash a chamois with soap.

Cleaning cloths are made from worn-out clothes, sheets, and towels. Cotton or linen fabrics that are white or light-colored are best.

Here are some quick tips to make this easy method for cleaning a room even easier:

- Carry two buckets or a bucket with two compartments when you are washing items that also need rinsing.

- Vacuum before cleaning with a liquid cleaning solution to avoid making mud.

- Go easy on cleaners. Soap or wax used sparingly clean and beautify surfaces. Use too much, and you will have to spend time removing the buildup and streaks.

- When cleaning something up high, don't stand on tiptoe: Grab a stepladder. If you are cleaning down low, sit on the floor. Straining up or down is tiring, inefficient, and bad for your back.

Rubber gloves only protect your hands if you wear them. Don't forget to put yours on whenever you work with cleaning solutions. Scouring pads are made of both synthetics and steel wool. Keep a variety in your cleaning closet. Sponges should be tossed out as soon as they start to shred. Have plenty on hand.

Stepladders, at least three feet tall, are a safe substitute for the unsteady chair or stack of boxes you may have been standing on to clean hard-to-reach places.

Mops should have detachable heads for easy cleaning.

Your **vacuum cleaner** with a set of cleaning tools and a **small handheld vacuum** are some of the most essential tools in your cleaning closet.

Window squeegees speed window washing, but if you don't have one, an old windshield wiper is a good stand-in for a commercial squeegee.

CLEANING AGENTS

In addition to your cleaning tools, you need to have on hand several basic cleaning supplies and the special cleaning agents for your Stain-Removal Kit.

All-purpose cleaners remove grease and grimy dirt.

Ammonia is available in clear or sudsy form. It is an excellent cleaner or cleaning booster for many household surfaces. It is a grease cutter, wax stripper, window cleaner, and general soil remover. If you object to the strong odor of ammonia, buy a scented product, but neither scented nor sudsy ammonia is suitable for stain removal.

Baking soda is one of the most versatile cleaning products available. Used by itself in dry form, it acts as a very mild scouring powder that will not scratch even the most delicate surfaces. Add water to make a paste, and use baking soda to scour dirty surfaces. Combined with other ingredients, it makes a very good cleaning solution that also deodorizes.

Bleach helps remove stains and whiten laundry, and it's also good for cleaning toilets. Flour is useful for some cleaning tasks. Always use flour in its dry form because it creates a gluey paste when mixed with water. Lemon juice, either

bottled or squeezed from a cut lemon, provides the mild acid reaction needed for many cleaning solutions.

Liquid dishwashing detergents are used for many cleaning tasks in addition to doing dishes.

Vinegar is also an acid; it can usually be substituted for lemon juice. **White vinegar** should be used to clean fabrics, but **cider vinegar** is adequate for other applications.

Waxes, **polishes**, and **oils** shine and protect wood, leather, brass, chrome, silver, glass, and other surfaces.

CHAPTER 2

Floors and Ceilings

Dirt from the street collects on feet and gets walked into your house a dozen times a day. The little dumps and spills of daily living accumulate with startling speed. These tips can help you handle every floor in your home in a fast, easy, no-hassle way.

CARPETS AND RUGS

For spilled popcorn, wayward crumbs, and crunched potato chips, a handheld vacuum will swoosh away the mess in seconds. But eventually you'll have to clean the entire floor. You can rely on an upright vacuum cleaner to clean carpets and rugs quickly and thoroughly.

VACUUMING YOUR CARPET

Later in this section, we'll talk about dealing with spots and stains, about specific cleaning techniques, and even about repairing carpets. But first, some general tips for carpet cleaning.

The easiest way to tackle a large job, like vacuuming a wall-to-wall-carpeted room, is to break it down into sections. When you mow the lawn, you make sure you go over all of it. When you vacuum wall-to-wall carpeting, you can be sure to cover every inch if you divide the floor into quarters. Vacuum an entire quarter before moving on to the next.

When you vacuum a carpet, especially a thick, plush carpet in which dirt is sure to be deeply embedded, take your time. One pass with even a high-powered upright is not enough. Go over each section of carpeting several times. Work slowly to allow the suction to remove all the ground-in dust and dirt. It's a good idea to vacuum your rugs and carpets about once a week, or more often in areas of heavy traffic. Frequent vacuuming prolongs the life of your carpet because it prevents a buildup of gritty particles that can cut carpet fibers. Every few weeks take a little extra time and use your crevice tool for in-depth cleaning around baseboards and radiators and in other hard-to-reach places.

When we say that you need to vacuum areas of heavy traffic frequently, we're not just talking about hallways and the route to the kitchen. People move their feet around when they sit and grind dirt from their shoes into the carpeting, so you'll need to pay special attention to the carpet in front of chairs and couches, and under desks. Vacuum areas of heavy traffic with a crisscross pattern of overlapping strokes.

A surefire way to cut your cleaning time in half is to put thick mats or throw rugs at all the entrances to your home, both inside and outside the doors. These mats intercept and trap loose dirt, keeping it from being tracked through your house. Compared with cleaning a whole room, throwing a washable rug into the washing machine or vacuuming a doormat takes practically no time at all.

After thoroughly vacuuming your rugs or carpet, you may find yourself faced with carpeting that is still not quite clean. Regular use of your vacuum cleaner will keep dirt from building up too fast, but eventually you'll need to deep-clean your carpet or have to deal quickly and effectively with spots and stains. Each kind of stain requires special treatment, and in this book you'll discover the best and quickest ways to clean up most kinds of spills. When it is time to deep-clean your carpet, turn to the section of this chapter that deals with shampooing carpet, and you'll find time-tested advice on the best, easiest, and fastest ways to clean.

BASIC CARPET CONSTRUCTION

Before you start to think about cleaning your carpet, let's consider the four major features that distinguish one carpet from another:

- **Fiber**

- **Pile and Density**

- **Padding**

- **Texture**

FIBER

Many people think that wool is the best carpet fiber when money is no object. But many synthetic fibers reproduce the natural qualities of wool, and some may resist stains better than wool does. Wool carpet releases soil easily, and it is resilient and does not support flame.

The quality of wool carpeting varies widely. Inferior wool carpets will shed, stain, and pill. A good synthetic carpet is better than inferior wool.

Most carpet sold in the United States is not made of wool but of synthetics. Nylon is the best synthetic carpet fiber. It is more durable and carefree than other man-made fibers. A well-constructed nylon carpet is an excellent investment.

Carpet made from synthetic fibers treated with special chemicals to resist stains may cost as much as good wool carpeting, but it may be worth the additional initial cost because it will look good for a long period of time.

Polyester and acrylic are less expensive carpet fibers. Because both of these kinds of fibers show soil and mat relatively quickly, they are best reserved for areas of low traffic.

Polypropylene (olefin) carpets are primarily used for basements and outdoor areas because the fiber resists moisture and fading.

PILE AND DENSITY

A carpet's performance is affected by its pile (carpet height) and density (number of tufts per square inch) as well as by its fiber content. High-pile carpeting may look especially soft and luxurious initially, but its height makes cleaning it difficult. The pile may "layover," causing people to walk on the sides of the yarn instead of on its surface. For most homes, high-density, low-pile carpeting will wear best. A good recommendation is a maximum pile height of .375 inches and a density of 64 tufts per square inch. Before you buy carpeting, give it a "palm test." This is a relatively accurate test of a carpet's wearability. Run the palm of your hand over the carpet's surface. If the fibers are flexible and bend easily, the carpet will wear out quickly. If the fibers resist the pressure from your hand, the carpet should wear well.

PADDING

Carpet padding does a lot more than put spring in your step when you walk across a carpeted room. Padding increases the life of a carpet by protecting the carpet backing that holds carpet fibers in place. Padding also absorbs noise and helps insulate a room from cold drafts.

Carpet padding is rated by weight. In most cases, thicker and heavier pads offer better protection than thinner and lighter pads. A minimum padding thickness of one-half inch is recommended.

TEXTURE

The texture of a carpet distinguishes one kind of carpeting from another. When carpeting is manufactured, loops of spun fiber are stitched through a backing. The loops can be cut and twisted to create various textures, or they can be left uncut. Varying the length of the loops or combining loops with cut pile creates a sculptured look.

Selecting the texture, fiber, and color of carpeting is a highly personal choice, but living with your choice and maintaining it may not be all that you had hoped if you do not choose wisely. A good-quality, thick-pile carpet in a combination of muted, dark tones is the best carpet choice for most homes.

Industrial-grade, tightly woven carpets not only wear like iron, but they feel like iron when you walk on them or kids play on them. Low-pile carpet, such as indoor/outdoor carpet, is

difficult to maintain because it shows dirt. A thick, plush carpet will hide dirt, but a short-pile, solid-color carpet reveals every speck of dirt and every tiny bit of litter, not to mention crumbs.

CARPET TREATMENTS

We all want to put off for as long a time as possible the day when we have to either deep-clean the carpet or move out of the house. In addition to using your vacuum cleaner regularly to keep dirt from becoming embedded in carpet fibers, experts have found that carpets treated to resist dirt and static really stay clean longer than untreated carpeting. We have also found a quick and effective treatment for a carpet that has picked up household or pet odors.

A soil retardant is a chemical treatment that coats carpet fibers to make them less able to absorb water- and oil-based spots and spills. Tea, milk, coffee, and winter slush are the main causes of carpet stains because they quickly soak into the carpet fibers and backing unless the carpet has been treated to resist soil.

Soil retardants can be applied to new carpets or to newly cleaned carpets. These chemicals may appear to be easy to apply, but heed the manufacturers' advice that you apply soil retardants only with professional equipment, using the recommended application techniques.

Carpets can also be treated with antistatic agents. This treatment will not only eliminate the irritation of mild electric shocks every time you touch a doorknob or a light switch, but it will also keep your home and carpet cleaner because static electricity has a magnetic effect on dust particles in the air.

There are many antistatic sprays on the market, but ordinary fabric softener works as well as many commercial antistatic products. Just as fabric softener takes static cling out of your laundry, it can remove static shock from your carpet. Spray your carpet lightly with a mixture of 5 parts water and 1 part liquid fabric softener. Be sure to let the carpet dry thoroughly before you walk on it. The result will be a shockless carpet.

Carpet odor can be eliminated without deep-cleaning. Try

sprinkling baking soda on the carpet before vacuuming. Or if you prefer, you can use 1 cup borax mixed with 2 cups cornmeal, but you must let this mixture stand on the carpet for at least an hour before vacuuming. Remember that these fine particles may stop the airflow through your vacuum's system sooner than larger dust particles, and a bag or canister that appears only partially filled may need to be changed or emptied. Don't forget to check any filters as well.

CLEANING SPILLS

You know that there is no way to prevent spills on carpeting, short of living in the kitchen. In many ways it's as easy, if not easier, to maintain a carpet as it is a hard-surface floor. If you treat spills quickly and correctly, most of them are not disastrous to your carpet. Prepare for the worst, stock up on the cleaning and stain-removing supplies you'll need, and then go ahead and paint your toenails in the bedroom, drink red wine in the living room, and let the kids make Christmas cards around the dining room table—your carpet really can take it. The secret of spot and stain removal is this: Clean spots and spills immediately. It's that simple. If you catch the spill when it's fresh, before it has become a stain, you've got a good chance of removing it totally. So when something spills, immediately move into action and follow this procedure:

- Carefully blot or scrape the entire stained area before

applying any cleaning solution. Remove as much of the spill as possible. If you just start right in cleaning, you'll make an even bigger mess because the cleaning solution you pour on will only spread the stain over more of the carpet.

- Before using any cleaning solution, test your carpet in an inconspicuous area to make sure the cleaner won't damage or discolor it. Since you want to move fast once a spill occurs, you should test the cleaning agents that you keep on hand before you have to use them to make sure that they will not harm your carpeting. (For example, you would not want to use any kind of acetone-based cleaner on acetate carpeting because it would dissolve the carpet fibers.)

- Do not rub the spill because rubbing might spread the problem to a larger area of the rug. When you apply spot cleaner, work from the outside of the stain toward the inside to avoid spreading the stain. You'll probably want to start cleaning the worst part of the stain first, but most substances stain as they dry. Cleaning the stain from the outside edges in toward the center gathers up the spill in order to get rid of it completely.

- After an application of a cleaning solution, blot up all the moisture. A clean, white bath towel is unsurpassed for drying carpet and brushing the nap back up to a standing position.

- After blotting the carpet, if you feel there is still too much moisture, place a ¼-inch-thick stack of white cloth towels over the spot and weight them with a heavy object.

Before applying cleaning solution, blot the stained area to remove as much of the spill as possible.

A GUIDE TO CARPET STAIN-REMOVAL

Experts have researched and completely tested the best and quickest methods for removing just about every kind of stain from just about every kind of surface. But we've found, as we're sure you know, that certain kinds of stains are more likely to happen to carpets than others.

So this is a quick-reference guide (in alphabetical order) to the best cures for the most common carpet spots and stains.

Acid Stains

Acid spills, such as toilet-bowl cleaner, drain cleaner, and vinegar, demand especially quick action. Dilute them immediately with baking soda and water or with club soda. You can tell by feel and smell when the acid spill has been cleaned up. Then apply a solution of ammonia (1 part) and water (10 parts). Rinse with cold water, let dry, and vacuum.

Alcoholic Beverages

If someone spills an alcoholic drink on your carpet, quickly dilute the spot with cold water so that the alcohol does not have time to attack the dyes. Absorb the excess liquid. Then mix 1 teaspoon mild detergent, 1 teaspoon white vinegar, and 1 quart warm water. Apply the solution to the spot. Let the carpet dry. If the spot remains, reapply the solution. Let the carpet dry completely. Vacuum gently.

Blood

Absorb as much of the blood as you can. Then mix 1 teaspoon mild detergent, 1 teaspoon white vinegar, and 1 quart warm water. Apply the solution to the spot. Let the carpet dry. Apply dry-cleaning fluid, and let the carpet dry completely before vacuuming.

Butter

The first step in cleaning up a butter spill is to scrape up as much solid butter as you can or to absorb all the melted butter that you can. Apply dry-cleaning fluid. Let the carpet dry. If the spot remains, reapply the fluid, and let the carpet dry thoroughly. Then vacuum.

Candle Wax

The easiest way to remove candle wax from your carpet is to press an ice cube against the drip. The wax will harden and can then be pulled off. Treat any remaining traces of wax with dry-cleaning fluid. Let the carpet dry, and vacuum.

Another way to remove candle wax on carpeting is to place a blotter over the spilled wax, and press with a warm iron until the blotter absorbs the melted wax. Move the blotter frequently so that it doesn't get oversaturated. Remove traces of the wax with spot remover.

Candy

Candy that contains no chocolate is usually easily removed from carpet. Scrape up as much of the candy as you can. Mix 1 teaspoon mild detergent, 1 teaspoon white vinegar, and 1 quart warm water. Apply the solution to the spot. Let the carpet dry. If the spot remains, reapply the solution. Let the carpet dry. Vacuum gently.

Chewing Gum

Chewing gum can be a sticky mess, so harden it by pressing an ice cube against the blob of gum. The gum will harden and can then be pulled off. Treat any remaining traces of the chewing gum with dry-cleaning fluid. Let the carpet dry, and then vacuum.

Chocolate

The longer chocolate is allowed to stay on your carpet, the more difficult it is to remove. Scrape the chocolate from the carpet. Mix 1 teaspoon mild detergent, 1 teaspoon white vinegar, and 1 quart warm water. Apply the solution to the spot. Rinse well with clear water, making sure you don't drench the carpet. Let the carpet dry. Vacuum gently.

Coffee

Blot spilled coffee immediately. Then mix 1 teaspoon mild detergent, 1 teaspoon white vinegar, and 1 quart warm water. Apply the solution to the spot. Let the carpet dry. Apply dry-cleaning fluid, and let the carpet dry again. Vacuum gently.

Crayon

Dropped crayons have a knack for getting stepped on and ground into carpeting. Scrape away excess crayon and remove the rest by placing a blotter over the crayon stain and pressing it with a warm iron until the blotter absorbs the melted crayon. Move the blotter frequently so that it doesn't get oversaturated. Apply dry-cleaning fluid, and let the carpet dry. Reapply if necessary, and then vacuum.

Egg

Like all protein stains, spilled eggs need to be cleaned up immediately. Scrape up as much cooked egg as possible or mop up raw egg. Mix 1 teaspoon mild detergent, 1 teaspoon white vinegar, and 1 quart warm water. Apply the solution to the spot. Let the carpet dry. If the spot remains, reapply the solution. Let the carpet dry. Vacuum gently.

Fruit

Fruit stains can be very hard to remove if they are allowed to set, but if you act quickly this method usually prevents a permanent stain. Scrape up spilled fruit, and absorb fruit juice. Mix 1 teaspoon mild detergent, 1 teaspoon white vinegar, and 1 quart warm water. Apply the solution to the spot. Let the carpet dry. If the spot remains, reapply the solution. Let the carpet dry. Vacuum gently.

Gravy

If you accidentally rock the gravy boat, wipe up as much of the spilled gravy as you can. Mix 1 teaspoon mild detergent, 1 teaspoon white vinegar, and 1 quart warm water. Apply the solution to the spot. Let the carpet dry. Apply dry-cleaning fluid. Let the carpet dry. Vacuum gently.

Hand Cream

When you inadvertently squirt

hand lotion on your carpet, wipe up the spill immediately. Apply dry-cleaning fluid. Let the carpet dry. If the spot remains, reapply the dry-cleaning fluid. Let the carpet dry, and then vacuum.

Ink

Fast action is essential when you spill ink on carpet. Immediately apply dry-cleaning fluid. Let the carpet dry. If the spot remains, reapply the dry-cleaning fluid. Let the carpet dry thoroughly, and vacuum.

Lipstick

When your carpet acquires a telltale trace of lipstick, scrape away as much of the lipstick as you can. Apply dry-cleaning fluid, and let it dry; then mix 1 teaspoon mild detergent, 1 teaspoon white vinegar, and 1 quart warm water. Apply the solution to the spot.

Let the carpet dry. If the spot remains, reapply the solution. Let the carpet dry. Vacuum gently.

Mildew

The first step in removing mildew stains is to kill the fungus. To do this, mix 1 teaspoon disinfectant cleaner and 1 cup water. Apply the solution to the mildewed carpet, and blot. To remove the stain, apply a solution of ammonia (1 part) and water (10 parts). Blot, rinse, and let dry. Vacuum. Keeping the area totally dry is the only way to prevent the reoccurrence of mildew, which can eventually break down carpet fibers.

Milk

Blot up the spilled milk. Mix 1 teaspoon mild detergent, 1 teaspoon white vinegar, and 1 quart warm water. Apply the solution to the spot. Let the carpet dry. Vacuum gently.

Mud

When muddy boots and shoes get past the mats at the entrances to your home, allow the mud tracked onto your carpeting to dry completely, and then brush or scrape off as much as possible. Mix 1 teaspoon mild detergent, 1 teaspoon white vinegar, and 1 quart warm water. Apply the solution to the spot. Let the carpet dry. If the stain remains, apply dry-cleaning fluid and blot dry. When the spot is completely dry, vacuum gently.

Nail Polish

Apply dry-cleaning fluid or amyl acetate, acetone, or nail-polish remover to the spilled polish. Test the solvent you plan to use on an inconspicuous part of the carpet. Never apply acetate, acetone, or nail-polish remover to acetate carpet fibers. If the stain remains, mix 1 teaspoon mild detergent, 1 teaspoon white vinegar, and 1 quart warm water. Apply the solution to the spot. Let the carpet dry. Vacuum gently.

Salad Dressing

A misplaced slosh of salad dressing can be removed easily from most carpeting. Absorb as much salad dressing as you can. Mix 1 teaspoon mild detergent, 1 teaspoon white vinegar, and 1 quart warm water. Apply the solution to the spot. Let the carpet dry. If the spot remains, reapply the solution. Let the carpet dry. Vacuum gently.

Tea

Tannic acid in black tea is a potent dye, so move quickly when tea is spilled. Blot up the tea spill. Mix 1 teaspoon mild detergent, 1 teaspoon white vinegar, and 1 quart warm water. Apply the solution to the spot. Let the carpet dry. Apply dry-cleaning fluid. Let the carpet dry. Vacuum gently.

Soft Drinks

The carbonation in soft drinks will help you clean spilled drinks quickly, but act fast because some of the dyes in the drinks can permanently stain your carpet. Blot up the spilled drink. Mix 1 teaspoon mild detergent, 1 teaspoon white vinegar, and 1 quart warm water. Apply the solution to the spot. Let the carpet dry. If the spot remains, reapply the solution. Let the carpet dry. Vacuum gently.

Urine

Mix 1 teaspoon mild detergent, 1 teaspoon white vinegar, and 1 quart warm water. Apply the solution to the spot. Let the carpet dry. If the spot remains, reapply the solution. Let the carpet dry. Vacuum gently.

Vomit

Treat vomit quickly. Blot up as much as possible, then dilute immediately with baking soda and water or with club soda. Then apply a solution of ammonia

(1 part) and water (10 parts). Rinse with cold water, let dry, and then vacuum.

Wine

When red wine is spilled on your carpet, dilute it with white wine, then clean the spot with cold water, and cover with table salt. Wait ten minutes, then vacuum up the salt.

SPECIAL PROBLEMS

When you look across the flawless expanse of a new carpet, you hate to think of all the potential disasters that lie ahead for your beautiful floor. Nevertheless, unexpected things will happen, and you may find yourself with especially stubborn carpet problems. Fortunately, we've learned how

to deal with them. When your carpet is burned, stained, or discolored, you can simply move a big chair over the spot and forget about it, or you can use one of these simple methods to restore your carpet to its original good looks:

• If the spot remover you use alters the color of your carpet, try touching up small places with artists' acrylic paint. If that doesn't work, try a permanent-ink or felt-tip marker of the appropriate color. Go slowly and blend the color into the fibers.

• To raise depressions left in carpet by heavy furniture, try steaming. Hold a steam iron close enough for steam to reach the carpet, but don't let the iron touch the fibers, especially if they are synthetic, because they could melt. Lift the fibers by scraping them with the edge of a coin or spoon.

- To repair a large burned area in a carpet, cut out the damaged area and substitute a patch of identical size and shape. Secure the new piece of carpeting with double-faced carpet tape or a latex adhesive.

- If a carpet thread is loose, snip it level with the pile. If you try to pull out the thread, you risk unraveling part of the carpet.

- To repair a small area burned down to the carpet backing, snip off the charred fibers, and put white glue in the opening. Then snip fibers from a scrap of carpet or an inconspicuous part of the carpet (perhaps in a closet). When the glue gets tacky, poke the fibers into place. If the burn isn't all the way down to the backing, just snip off the charred tips of the fibers with scissors. The slightly shorter length of a few carpet fibers will never be noticed.

DEEP-CLEANING CARPETS

There comes a time in the life of every carpet when vacuuming can no longer restore its clean appearance. Since you don't want to rush into a major cleaning job, try the following checklist for dirty carpets. If any of these descriptions fit your carpet, then it is time to deep-clean it.

- The carpet is matted and feels sticky to bare feet.

- The carpet is no longer the same color as the remnant you saved when the carpet was new.

- The carpet has grimy circles around the chairs where people sit to read or watch TV.

- The carpet releases a dust storm when you run across the room to answer the phone.

You should have your carpet professionally cleaned unless you have the time and patience to do a thorough cleaning job. One of the reasons that many people believe that carpets soil faster after they have been shampooed is that some people clean only the surface of their carpeting when they think they are deep-cleaning it. The only method that cleans carpeting down to the backing is to agitate it with a shampooer and rinse it with an extractor.

Should you decide to rent carpet-cleaning equipment and shampoo your carpets yourself, we suggest that you allow plenty of uninterrupted time for the task. This is a very big job, and rushing it will mean disappointing results. To speed drying, you should also plan to shampoo carpets during dry periods of the year or when the heating system is operating.

Before cleaning your carpeting, we recommend that you test for colorfastness. Moisten a white towel with the cleaning solution that you are going to be using and apply it to an inconspicuous area. If the towel does not pick up any color from the carpet, it is probably safe to use the solution on the entire carpet.

Remove as much furniture from the room as possible, and place foil or plastic film under the legs and bases of the remaining furniture to prevent stains. (The foil or plastic should be left in place until the carpet is completely dry.) Vacuum the carpet thoroughly, then spot-clean and pretreat stains before shampooing the carpet. Always follow the instructions printed on the carpet cleaner you rent, but here are a few additional hints that we hope will make shampooing your carpet easier.

- Use single strokes over the carpet surface.

- Do not apply heavy pressure with the machine.

- Wipe cleaner solutions and foam from woodwork and furniture immediately to prevent damage to the wood or upholstery.

- Fluff damp fibers against the nap after shampooing to aid drying and prevent any matting.

- Make sure the room is well ventilated after cleaning to speed drying.

- Try not to walk on carpets until they are dry.

SURFACE-CLEANING CARPETS

It may be possible for you to put off shampooing your carpets almost indefinitely if you are willing to spend extra time each month to keep them clean. Here is an adaptation of a carpet-cleaning method sometimes used by professional cleaners to clean the surface dirt from carpets. This is not a deep-cleaning operation. It is a carpet-maintenance technique intended to prevent carpets from needing a major shampooing too often.

If you vacuum your carpets frequently, most dirt accumulates on top of the carpet fibers and is not transferred to the backing. Moisten a two-inch-thick pad, made from a Turkish towel or other heavy-duty cloth, with carpet-cleaning solution, and wring out the excess moisture in a roller mop bucket. Mount the pad on a household floor polisher and run it over the carpet. The pad picks up and absorbs surface grime and soil. When the cloth becomes dirty, turn it over and repeat the process. When both sides are dirty, rinse the pad in the mop bucket, wring, and repeat.

RUG CARE

With the following exceptions, it is suggested that you clean and maintain rugs in exactly the same way you take care of carpets. Remember to vacuum both the top and bottom surfaces of a rug to keep dirt particles from wearing out rug fibers. The following collection of hints will help you care for rugs that need special care:

Natural Fibers: After vacuuming the surface and underneath fiber, sisal, and grass rugs, remove dirt and restore moisture to the rugs with a damp cloth.

Fur: Clean fur rugs by working multiple applications of

cornmeal through the pile until the cornmeal shakes out clean. Then lightly vacuum the remaining granules. A fur rug can also be spot-cleaned with a damp cloth, but don't get the pelt wet.

Washable Fibers: Air dry round or oval throw rugs to retain their shape, but don't hang them over a clothesline; dry them flat.

HARD-SURFACE FLOORS

Hard-surface floors come in a variety of materials. In this section, we'll discuss some tips for taking care of the most common kinds of hard-surface floors.

VACUUMING HARD-SURFACE FLOORS

Unlike other methods of attacking the dirt that piles up on hard-surface floors, using your vacuum cleaner doesn't just push dirt around. Whether it's a handheld vacuum or an upright canister, your vacuum cleaner gets dirt off your hard-surface floors and puts it neatly in a bag or container so it's ready to be taken out of your home for good.

Vacuuming hard-surface floors before you wash them saves you time because when you wash or polish the floor there is no dirt to grind into the floor covering or turn to mud. To not only speed up cleaning but get your home really clean, always vacuum the floor before you clean it with water or wax.

It is recommended that you vacuum your wood and other hard-surface floors about once a week, more often in areas of heavy traffic or if the floor is dark or very shiny. Lint and dust show up faster on polished surfaces than they do on carpeting, so use a handheld or lightweight cordless vacuum between regular cleanings to keep your floor sparkling with a minimum of effort. Frequent vacuuming prolongs the life of the floor because it prevents a buildup of grit that can scratch hard-surface flooring.

The techniques you use to vacuum a carpeted room should also be used when you vacuum an uncarpeted room. Never use an upright or power team powerhead on a hard-surface floor; both the vacuum and the floor are likely to be damaged permanently. A canister, power team, or upright vacuum with a floor-nozzle attachment or a lightweight cordless vacuum is best for removing dust and debris from all hard-surface floors. Thoroughly vacuum, going back and forth across each section. Two slow strokes are usually sufficient to pick up the loose dirt. (Use a small-brush attachment to clean around baseboards and radiators and in other hard-to-reach places.)

CLEANING HARD-SURFACE FLOORS

There are probably many different kinds of hard-surface floors in your home. Your vacuum cleaner can help you maintain all the floors in your home, from the concrete in your basement to the parquet under the rug in the living room. Unfortunately, weekly vacuuming is not all it takes to keep a hard-surface floor looking its best. So here are a few quick and easy cleaning methods to help you speed through the heel marks and the sticky stuff that accumulate on your hard-surface floors.

Whenever you go to the grocery or hardware store, you will find an array of specialized cleaning products. Many commercial products are very good at cleaning what they are designed to clean. Which products you use to clean your floors is entirely up to you. We have included some tried-and-true recipes for cleaners that can be made from products you're likely to have in your cupboards. These solutions and methods don't

necessarily work better than commercial products, but they all work as well. We know; we've tested them. So if you have time to clean your bathroom floor, but you've run out of the cleaner you usually use, try the homemade remedy. It will save you money, and it will save you time, since you won't have to run out to the store before you start to clean.

Asphalt Tile

An asphalt-tile floor won't retain leg imprints when you replace your old favorite TV chair in the family room with a snazzy new one. But even though asphalt tile recovers well from indentations, we suggest that you use plastic, not rubber, casters and cups on furniture legs to minimize scratches and indentations. Although asphalt is resilient, you should know that grease, oil, and solvents—such as kerosene, gasoline, naphtha, and turpentine—or harsh cleaning preparations and strong soaps as well as scouring can leave the surface of your floor looking like the moon.

ASPHALT-FLOOR CLEANER AND POLISH

Mix ½ cup vinegar, 2 tablespoons furniture polish, and 1 gallon warm water.

Caution: Wear rubber gloves. Mop the floor with this mixture, using a sponge mop or string mop.

If you take the time to damp mop your asphalt floor every week, you will not have to wash and polish it as often as if you allow dirt to build up. Make sure that the cleaner or polish you use can withstand damp mopping. If it can't, you will have to reapply it. We've found that adding a cup of fabric softener to a half pail of water will prevent damp mopping from dulling the shine on your floor.

When you decide to wash the floor, don't flood the floor with water; excess water can seep into the seams and loosen adhesives that hold down the flooring.

Remove heel marks by dipping fine-grade (OOO) steel wool in liquid floor wax and rubbing the spot gently. Wipe with a damp cloth.

The *fastest* way to clean an asphalt floor is with a one-step cleaner/polish. If you use a commercial water-based polish, don't shake it before use.

The *best* way we've found to clean an asphalt floor takes longer than using a one-step, but it gives an asphalt-tile floor a more durable finish than other cleaning methods.

Mix $\frac{1}{4}$ cup low-sudsing, all-purpose cleaner; 1 cup ammonia; and $\frac{1}{2}$ gallon cool or cold water. **Caution:** Wear rubber gloves and work in a well-ventilated area when using this powerful solution. Apply the cleaner to the floor with a sponge mop, using pressure for heavily soiled areas. Rinse with cool, clear water for spotless results. Apply two thin coats of a water-based, self-polishing floor finish, allowing the floor to dry between coats. Apply the polish with a long-handled wax applicator that has a washable chenille pad.

Brick

Your brick floor may appear to be very durable because of its hard, fired surface. But in reality brick is porous and stains easily. For this reason, the best way to care for your brick floor is to keep it sealed and waxed.

You'll need to use a commercial sealer for brick.

Damp mopping with a sponge mop or string mop after vacuuming will prevent dirt from building up on your brick floor, so you can put off washing and/or stripping the floor. Try adding a cup of vinegar to the mop water; the floor will glisten without being polished—a real time-saver.

If you use a water-based, self-polishing liquid wax, you'll occasionally have to strip the wax buildup before you rewax. Use a solvent-based wax so that you don't have to strip your floor. A solvent-based polish can be applied over a water-based polish, but a water-based polish cannot be applied over a solvent-based polish. The solvents in the wax dissolve the layer of wax that is on the floor every time solvent-based wax is applied, so there is no wax buildup.

If your floor has a wax buildup, you can remove it by applying a wax-stripping product with a scrub brush or floor-scrubbing machine that has a brush attachment. Rinse the floor thoroughly with clear water after applying the stripper according to the manufacturer's directions. Do not clean your brick floor with acids, strong soaps, or abrasives.

Caring for a porous brick floor is a lot of work no matter what you do. If you use a solvent-based wax on the floor, you have to seal it. If you use a water-based polish, you'll occasionally have to strip the wax buildup.

While the following method of caring for a brick floor is not as effective as a treatment with stripper, sealer, and paste wax, it is a quick and inexpensive way to take care of your brick floor. Since this homemade solution contains ammonia, you strip the floor every time you wash it, eliminating wax buildup. Most acrylic liquid waxes are self-sealing, allowing you to skip the application of a sealer. Clean and strip the floor with a solution of $1/4$ cup low-sudsing, all-purpose cleaner; 1 cup clear ammonia; and $1/2$ gallon cool or cold water. **Caution:** Wear rubber gloves, and work in a well-ventilated area when using this powerful solution. Apply the solution to the floor with a sponge mop, using pressure for heavily soiled areas; rinse with cool, clear water for spotless results. Then apply two thin coats of an acrylic floor wax.

Ceramic Tile, Glazed

Before there was vinyl, there was glazed ceramic tile for people like us who quickly say no, thank you, when it comes to complicated and time-consuming cleaning projects. Highly glazed ceramic tile is an almost carefree floor covering. It requires little more than regular vacuuming and damp mopping.

We suggest that you damp mop with an all-purpose cleaner, using a synthetic scouring pad and nonabrasive cleaner for stubborn spots. Then dry the floor with a soft cloth to avoid streaks. If the freshly mopped floor dries with a luster-dulling film, mop it again with water containing a cup of white vinegar, and the floor will glisten.

Ceramic Tile, Unglazed

Unlike shiny, easy-to-care-for glazed tile, unglazed ceramic tile is porous and must be sealed to resist stains. Your new unglazed ceramic-tile floor needs to be sealed with a commercial sealer and a water-based wax.

Damp mopping with a sponge mop or string mop after you vacuum will allow you to put off washing and rewaxing the floor until it is really dirty. We've discovered that if you put a cup of vinegar in the mop water, your unglazed ceramic tile floor will glisten.

About once a year, you will need to strip the wax buildup on your tile floor and rewax. A floor-scrubbing machine that has a brush attachment really saves time on this job, but if you don't have or can't rent a machine, a scrub brush can be used to apply the wax-stripping product. Rinse the floor thoroughly with clear water after applying the stripper. Do not clean your unglazed ceramic-tile floor with acids, strong soaps, or abrasives.

When you rewax the floor, you can use either a water-based, self-polishing wax or a paste wax. We recommend that you use the following homemade solution in conjunction with a water-based, acrylic self-polishing wax. This

method is not as effective as a treatment with stripper, sealer, and paste wax, but we have found that it works nearly as well, and it's quick and inexpensive.

Clean and strip the floor with a solution of $1/4$ cup low-sudsing, all-purpose cleaner; 1 cup clear ammonia; and $1/2$ gallon cool or cold water. **Caution:** Wear rubber gloves and work in a well-ventilated area when using this powerful solution. Apply the solution to the floor with a sponge mop, using pressure for heavily soiled areas; rinse with cool, clear water for spotless results. Then apply two thin coats of an acrylic floor wax.

Concrete

If you're like most people, you probably put off dealing with the concrete floors in your unfinished basement and garage for as long as possible. The result is that they get really dirty because concrete is very porous and soaks up stains quickly. While few of us are so fastidious as to seal or paint our garage floors, the time you take to seal a basement floor, especially if it is new, will save time in the long run, since the sealed floor will require little more cleaning than vacuuming. When your basement floor does have to be washed, go ahead and get it really clean by washing it with a strong, all-purpose cleaning solution.

After you have gotten rid of the loose surface dirt, we suggest you use the homemade cleaning solution given here. It works as well as a commercial heavy-duty cleaner, and it's much less expensive.

Garage floors are not a pretty scene. They soak up oil and grease stains,

gather piles of litter, and collect dirt. But not many people spend much time in the garage, so you don't need to attack the mess very often.

CLEANER FOR CONCRETE

Mix 1/4 cup low-sudsing, all-purpose cleaner; 1 cup clear ammonia; and 1/2 gallon cool or cold water.

Caution: Wear rubber gloves, and work in a well-ventilated area when using this powerful solution. Apply to the concrete floor with a sponge mop, using pressure for heavily soiled areas; rinse with cool, clear water for spotless results. Let the floor dry.

We suggest that you spread kitty litter to absorb oil and grease and that you keep the garage door closed so that leaves and other windblown debris don't collect in your garage.

When it comes time to clean the garage floor, sweep out the dirt, dust, and kitty litter with a stiff broom. You should work from the back of the garage to the front. Then get out the garden hose, and flush the floor with clear water. You can scour tough globs of dirt with your stiff broom or blast them with a jet of water.

Cork

A cork floor recovers quickly from the pressure of chair legs and the wear and tear of heavy foot traffic, but water will do it in every time; even the small amount of H_2O in water-based cleaners is too much wet for a cork floor. You must use only solvent-based cleaners and polishes to maintain cork-tile flooring.

A new cork floor should be sealed with varnish, shellac, or lacquer. Paint or lacquer thinner, alcohol, and other chemicals will damage these sealers, so try not to use them near the floor.

You can remove heel marks from a cork floor by applying a solvent-based wax, polish, or cleaner to a rag and rubbing the mark.

The fastest way to clean a cork floor is with a one-step product specifically formulated to clean and polish cork floors. Sadly, the fastest way is not the best way to care for cork. If your floor is new or a focal point of your home, you should take the time twice a year to clean the floor with a liquid wood-floor cleaning product and to rewax. Use a liquid cleaner/wax that soaks into the floor. Wipe up the excess liquid, and allow the floor to dry, then buff it with a floor polisher.

The second step of this process is to apply a liquid or paste solvent-based wax. No stripping will ever be necessary because the solvents in the new wax will strip off the old wax. Shake solvent-based liquid polishes vigorously before use. All you have to do to renew the shine between cleanings is to buff the floor when it appears dull.

Flagstone and Slate

These natural-stone flooring materials are similar in that they have rough, porous surfaces and are set into grout. This type of flooring wears like rock, but it will look like it should have been left outside if it is not cared for properly. Flagstone and slate floors must be sealed with a commercial sealer, not lacquer or varnish.

The best way to seal a flagstone or slate floor is with a sealer for terrazzo and slate. After the sealer dries, apply two thin coats of an acrylic floor finish with a long-handled wax applicator fitted with a lamb's wool pad, or apply paste wax with a floor-polishing machine. To do this, use a spatula to spread a small amount of paste wax directly on the brushes of the polisher. Slowly operate the polisher back and forth to apply an even, thin coat of wax. When dry, buff the floor.

A self-polishing liquid will build up on your floor, and you'll occasionally have to strip the wax buildup and rewax. Applying a wax-stripping product with a scrub brush will work, but using a floor-scrubbing machine that has a brush attachment will keep you off your knees. After applying the stripper according to the manufacturer's directions, rinse the floor thoroughly with clear water. Then apply wax to the floor.

To keep ahead of dirt, damp mop flagstone or slate floors with a sponge mop or string mop, using clear water, an all-purpose cleaning solution in warm water, or water to which fabric softener has been added. Wring the mop until it doesn't drip, and apply it to the floor in slow, even strokes with just enough pressure to loosen and pick up dirt. If the freshly mopped floor dries with a luster-dulling film, you can mop it again with water containing a cup of white vinegar; the floor will glisten.

CLEANER FOR FLAGSTONE AND SLATE

Mix ¼ cup low-sudsing, all-purpose cleaner; 1 cup clear ammonia; and ½ gallon cool or cold water.

Caution: Wear rubber gloves, and work in a well-ventilated area when using this powerful solution. Apply to the floor with a sponge mop, using pressure for heavily soiled areas. Rinse the floor thoroughly with clean water. Apply sealer, then buff.

Linoleum

Sad but true, linoleum must be waxed to shine and stand up to foot traffic effectively. But once it is waxed, the only regular maintenance a linoleum floor needs is vacuuming and an occasional swipe with a damp mop. A cup of vinegar in the mop water will bring up the shine on the floor, so you can delay rewaxing until it's really necessary.

Remove heel marks from linoleum by dipping fine-grade (OOO) steel wool in liquid floor wax. Rub the spot gently, and wipe with a damp cloth.

A water-based cleaner/polish or an all-purpose cleaning solution is best for the routine care of a linoleum floor. Solvent-based products can soften and damage linoleum. Scouring the floor, flooding it with water, or using very hot water or strong soaps are other no-nos for linoleum floors.

The fastest way to clean a linoleum floor is with a one-step cleaner/polish, but the best way to clean the floor is to mop it with an all-purpose cleaner. Dissolve the cleaner in very warm water, rinse, and apply two thin coats (let dry between coats) of a water-based, self-polishing liquid. Use a long-handled wax applicator fitted with a washable chenille pad.

LINOLEUM CLEANER/POLISH

Mix 1/2 cup vinegar, 2 tablespoons furniture polish, and 1 gallon cool or cold water.

Caution: Wear rubber gloves. Mop the floor with this mixture, using a sponge or string mop.

Occasionally, you'll have to remove wax buildup with an all-purpose cleaner or stripper. We recommend that you always test a corner of the floor before stripping the whole thing to make sure the product you're using won't permanently damage the flooring.

Marble

Marble flooring is available in a variety of colors, with a polished or nonpolished finish, and in an array of thicknesses and shapes. Nonpolished marble is very porous, stains easily, and must be sealed with a commercial sealer. Don't use varnish or lacquer to seal marble; it quickly peels off. Polished marble is less porous but can still be stained; we recommend a commercial marble sealer for this finish also.

Marble floors look great after being damp mopped with a sponge mop or string mop, using clear water, an all-purpose cleaning solution in warm water, or a mixture of 1 cup fabric softener and ½ gallon water. Wring the mop until it doesn't drip, and apply the mixture to the floor in slow, even strokes with just enough pressure to loosen and pick up dirt. If the mopped floor dries with a luster-dulling film, mop it again with water containing a cup of white vinegar. The floor will glisten—it sure beats rewaxing.

Water-based, self-polishing liquid wax is a fast, shiny finish for marble. There's only one problem with using it: Occasionally, you'll have to strip the wax buildup and rewax. Applying a wax-stripping product with a floor-scrubbing machine with a brush attachment makes the job slightly more pleasant than crawling around on your knees with a scrub brush. After applying the stripper according to the manufacturer's directions, rinse the floor thoroughly with clear water. Then apply wax to the floor.

You can use either a water-based self-polishing wax or a paste wax. If you use a water-based polish, don't shake it before use. A solvent-based polish can be applied over a water-based polish, but a water-based polish cannot be applied over a solvent-based polish. If you use a paste wax, test it in a corner to see if it will discolor the flooring. If a solvent-based paste wax is used, rewax to strip the old wax and to renew the shine.

Quarry Tile

Like brick, quarry tile looks durable, but this unglazed clay tile is really very porous and readily soaks up stains. Quarry-tile floors have to be well sealed with as many as three coats of sealer and further protected by a high-quality wax. Our years of experience in cleaning floors have failed to turn up a truly easy way to seal a quarry-tile floor. But if you do it right, you won't have to do it very often.

The best way we have found to seal a quarry-tile floor is with a commercial sealer for terrazzo and slate. After the sealer dries, apply two thin coats of an acrylic floor finish, using a long-handled wax applicator fitted with a lamb's wool pad, or apply paste wax with a floor-polishing machine. To do this, use a spatula to spread a small amount of paste wax directly on the brushes of the polisher. Slowly operate the polisher back and forth to apply an even, thin coat of wax. When the wax is dry, buff the floor.

To keep your sealed-and-waxed quarry-tile floor looking really terrific, all you have to do is damp mop it occasionally after you vacuum. If the mopped floor dries with a luster-dulling film, you can restore the shine by mopping it again with water containing a cup of white vinegar.

When it comes time to strip the wax buildup and rewax, apply a commercial wax-stripping product with a floor-scrubbing machine that has a brush attachment. After applying the stripper according to the manufacturer's directions, rinse the floor thoroughly with clear water. Use a nonabrasive powder and a synthetic scouring pad for stubborn spots.

If you plan to use a paste wax, such as those used on wood floors, test the wax in a corner to see if it will discolor the tile. You will never have to strip the wax. Rewaxing will strip the old wax and renew the shine.

Rubber Tile

Rubber tile is slightly delicate; it can be damaged by exposure to direct sunlight, and it is easily wrecked by strong cleaners. Care for rubber tile in much the same way that you maintain asphalt tile, but you'll have to be a little more careful.

No one has time to wash floors on a weekly basis, but most of us can find time to pass a damp mop over the floor after we've vacuumed it. This will delay for a long time the day when you finally have to mop. A trick we've found to make a rubber-tile floor look freshly waxed is to add a cup of fabric softener to a half pail of water. This prevents damp mopping from dulling the shine on your floor. Also, be sure

that you use a cleaner/polish that can withstand damp mopping; if it can't, you'll end up reapplying the cleaner/polish every time you mop.

The quickest way we have found to clean a rubber-tile floor is to use a water-based cleaner/polish or an all-purpose cleaning solution. It is recommended that you read the product label for precautionary measures and test any cleaner in a corner before using it on the entire floor.

Occasionally, remove wax buildup with a cleaner or wax stripper. Follow stripping with two thin coats of self-polishing wax; allow to dry between coats. Two thin coats make a much more durable, long-lasting finish than one coat, which may dry slowly and leave a gummy, dust-collecting mess on your floor.

Remove heel marks from rubber tile by dipping fine-grade (OOO) steel wool in liquid floor wax. Rub the spot gently, and wipe with a damp cloth.

Solvent-based products can soften and damage a rubber-tile floor. Also, keep scouring pads, strong soaps, and hot water away from rubber tile.

Flooding the floor with water will also cause big problems; excess water can seep into the seams and loosen the adhesives that hold down the flooring.

CLEANER/POLISH FOR RUBBER TILE

Mix 1/2 cup vinegar, 2 tablespoons furniture polish, and 1 gallon warm water.

Caution: Wear rubber gloves. Mop the floor with this mixture, using a sponge or string mop.

Terrazzo

Terrazzo is a very durable floor that was once used only in schools and other public buildings, but is now showing up in bathrooms and entrance halls in homes. This flooring is made of marble chips set in cement. After it cures, terrazzo is ground and polished. As durable as it seems, we have found that terrazzo stains easily and must be sealed with a commercial sealer, not with varnish or lacquer.

We've found that the best way to seal a terrazzo floor is with a commercial sealer for terrazzo and slate. After the sealer dries, apply two thin coats of an acrylic floor finish, using a long-handled wax applicator fitted with a lamb's wool pad, or apply paste wax with a floor-polishing machine. To do this, use a spatula to spread a small amount of paste wax directly on the brushes of the polisher. Slowly operate the polisher back and forth to apply an even, thin coat of wax. When the wax is dry, buff the floor.

After you have gone to the trouble to properly seal your terrazzo floor, it will reward you by being very easy to care for. All a terrazzo floor needs to keep it looking good is a quick going over with a damp mop, using clear water, an all-purpose cleaner in warm water, or a mixture of 1 cup fabric softener and 1/2 gallon water. If your mopped floor dries with a luster-dulling film, we've discovered that if you quickly mop it again with water containing a cup of white vinegar, the floor will glisten.

Occasionally, you'll have to strip the wax buildup on your floor and rewax if you use a water-based, self-polishing liquid. Apply a

commercial wax-stripping product with a floor-scrubbing machine that has a brush attachment. After applying the stripper according to the manufacturer's directions, rinse the floor thoroughly with clear water. A nonabrasive powder and a synthetic scouring pad will remove stubborn spots without scratching the floor.

Vinyl

Vinyl floor coverings are ideal for everyone who hates to clean. They are truly easy-care, and there are many excellent products on the market that are designed to maintain a sparkling vinyl floor in one quick step.

If you don't want to use one of these products, the best way to clean a vinyl-tile floor is with an all-purpose cleaner dissolved in water. After you have cleaned the floor, rinse the tile with clear water to make sure no film remains to dull the finish. When the floor is dry, apply two thin coats of water-based, self-polishing floor finish, allowing the floor to dry between coats. Apply the wax with a long-handled wax applicator fitted with a washable chenille pad.

CLEANER/POLISH FOR VINYL

Mix ½ cup vinegar, 2 tablespoons furniture polish, and 1 gallon warm water.

Caution: Wear rubber gloves. Mop the floor with this mixture, using a sponge or string mop.

It will be a long time before you need to do anything more for your floor than to wipe up spills and vacuum. But if you want to damp mop after vacuuming, add a cup of fabric softener to a half pail of water to prevent damp mopping from dulling the shine on your vinyl floor.

Remove heel marks from vinyl floors by dipping a synthetic scouring pad in liquid floor wax. Rub the spot gently and wipe with a damp cloth.

Vinyl, "No-Wax"

A "no-wax" vinyl floor is a breeze to maintain. All you have to do is keep it clean, and damp mopping after vacuuming goes a long way toward doing that. Obviously, you don't have time to mop the kitchen floor after dinner every day, so go ahead and wipe up spills with a sponge dipped in dishwashing liquid, scrub off heel marks with a synthetic scouring pad, and put off washing the floor until it gets really sticky, if you want to.

When it's finally time to wash the floor, use an all-purpose cleaning solution. Always be sure to read the product label for precautionary measures and instructions. We have also found that it pays to test any cleaner in a corner before using it on the entire floor.

Sometimes a "no-wax" floor dries with a luster-dulling film; don't panic, just mop it again with water containing a cup of white vinegar, and the floor will glisten like new.

If your "no-wax" floor loses its shine in high-traffic areas, use a gloss-renewing product available from the manufacturer of your floor or another commercial product designed for this purpose. Never throw just anything you have around the house on the dull floor: Solvent-based products or cleaners that contain pine oil can soften and permanently damage a vinyl-tile floor. Also, do not scour

"no-wax" vinyl, use strong soaps and hot water, or flood the floor with water. Excess water can seep into the seams and loosen the adhesives that hold down the flooring.

Wood

There is almost nothing as elegant as a glimmering wood floor. The sight of such a floor speaks to us of glamour, good living, and a lot of very hard work on somebody's part (preferably not yours). It's true that you have to take care of a wood floor, but you don't have to break your back to do it if you care for it our way.

The product used to seal a wood floor determines how it can be cared for. Varnish, polyurethane, shellac, and lacquer are used to finish floors, but only polyurethane requires no further treatment, including waxing. The integrity and beauty of wood floors not finished with polyurethane can be maintained only by using solvent-based cleaners and polishes. Water should never be used on wood floors, except those treated with polyurethane; these can be damp mopped. If you have the choice and don't want to spend your time maintaining your wood floor, we recommend that you have your wood floors finished with polyurethane.

If you have lacquered, varnished, or shellacked floors, the fastest way to clean a wood floor is with a one-step cleaner/polish. After vacuuming the floor, pour the solvent-based liquid on a small area and rub lightly with a clean, dry wax applicator. Working on a small section at a time, stroke the floor in the direction of the grain.

Blot up any excess liquid with a clean cloth.

To achieve a long-lasting shine on your wood floor, you will have to spend more time and follow this tested method. After vacuuming the floor, apply a liquid wood-floor cleaner with a dry wax applicator or a cloth on a small area at a time. Let it soak for 3 minutes, and wipe up the excess. When the floor is dry, buff with a floor polisher. **Caution:** This is a combustible mixture; use in a well-ventilated area.

Unless you always take off your shoes at the door, you'll probably have to apply a liquid or paste solvent-based wax to your wood floor about twice a year. No stripping is necessary because the solvents in the new wax will strip off the old wax. Make sure the room is well ventilated when using solvent-based waxes and polishes.

CEILINGS

Most of us ignore our ceilings, but when we finally look up, we're likely to see a grayish, brownish haze, combining the smoke of burned toast with cooking grease and all kinds of airborne particles. If your ceiling has lost its original color, you'll have to brush away the cobwebs and wipe away the smog. It's not something you need to do very often, but we're here to help you when the time comes.

Acoustical Tile and Suspended Panel

Acoustical ceiling treatments are made of porous materials to absorb noise. You can wash

Here are some basic tips to make ceiling cleaning easier:

- Lift cobwebs off ceilings with your vacuum cleaner and its brush attachment. Be careful not to crush cobwebs onto the ceiling; they will leave black smudge marks.

- Wash or clean ceilings before walls if you are cleaning the whole room. But watch out for drips; if you allow drips to run down walls, they may leave permanent marks.

- Protect furniture and floors with plastic drop cloths or newspaper while you clean the ceiling.

- Use a sponge mop to clean ceilings so you won't need a ladder.

vinyl-coated acoustical ceilings. Use an all-purpose cleaning solution applied with a sponge mop. Noncoated tiles generally are not washable, but you can spot-clean them, using special products available at hardware stores. When an overall cleaning is needed, we recommend an application of acoustical-tile paint.

Tile

Vinyl-coated ceiling tile can be cleaned with an all-purpose cleaning solution. Nonwashable tiles can be spot-cleaned with products available at most hardware and paint stores. When an overall cleaning is needed, paint the tiles with either latex or oil-based paint.

Painted

The most frequently used ceiling paint is latex, which is easy to wash after it has "cured," or set for a period of time. The other kind of paint used on ceiling is alkyd, or oil-based; it is durable and washable and comes in three finishes: flat, semigloss, and gloss. Flat and semigloss are most often used on ceilings, but some bathroom and kitchen ceilings are gloss.

PAINTED-CEILING CLEANER

Mix $1/2$ cup vinegar, 1 cup clear ammonia, $1/4$ cup baking soda, and 1 gallon warm water.

Caution: Wear rubber gloves, and work in a well-ventilated area when using this solution. Apply it to the ceiling with a sponge and rinse with clear water.

Be sure to clean painted ceilings with commercial liquid or powdered all-purpose cleaners. Always follow the manufacturer's instructions, rinse with clear water, and allow to dry.

Papered

Paper-covered ceilings are not washable. When you need to clean them, we recommend that you use a commercial wallpaper cleaning product and follow the manufacturer's instructions for the best results.

We've found that you can remove smudges from papered ceilings by very gently rubbing the spots with an art gum eraser. General soil comes off when a piece of rye bread is wadded up and used like an eraser.

To clean a grease spot, blot it with paper towels and gently press cornstarch on the stain. After the cornstarch absorbs the grease, rub it off gently.

VINYL-COVERED CEILING CLEANERS

Mix ½ cup vinegar and 1 quart water. Gently apply the solution to the ceiling with a sponge.

Caution: Wear rubber gloves when you work with this cleaner. Don't let the ceiling get too wet; moisture could seep under the seams and loosen the backing of the vinyl.

- OR -

You can make a "dry detergent" to clean vinyl ceiling coverings. Mix ¼ cup dishwashing liquid with 1 cup warm water in a mixing bowl and beat the solution with an eggbeater to a stiff foam. Working in a small area, dip a sponge into the foam and apply it to the ceiling to loosen dirt. Rinse the detergent with a sponge dipped in clear water and squeezed dry.

Many ceilings are "papered" with washable vinyl. Some manufacturers of vinyl wall-coverings caution against using ammonia-based cleaners. Be sure to check the instructions for cleaning your particular ceiling, or test your ceiling covering in an inconspicuous area before you attempt to clean the entire surface.

Plaster

Decorative plaster ceilings, as opposed to flat, painted plaster ceilings, can't be cleaned because of their unpainted surface and deep texture. When a plaster ceiling becomes dirty, the best treatment is first to vacuum it, using a brush attachment on your vacuum cleaner, and then to respray it with plaster.

Spray-on Acoustical Finish

This rough, sound-absorbing finish is often used in new construction and remodeling. Spray-on acoustical finishes are relatively inexpensive and quick to apply. They cover cracks and other ceiling imperfections. But this kind of ceiling can't be cleaned. When the ceiling becomes dirty, the best thing to do is to vacuum it, using a brush attachment on your vacuum cleaner. Then respray it with a thin coat of the original finish. Spray equipment is available to rent at most paint stores.

CHAPTER 3
Walls and Windows

Bathroom and kitchen messes are unique, and we clean these rooms in special ways. But the other rooms of our homes are pretty much the same—rectangular cubes that collect dirt, clutter, grease stains, and dirty socks. When it comes to cleaning, a wall is a wall; it's not a family-room wall or a living-room wall. This is not to say that all walls are cleaned in the same way. There are painted walls, papered walls, vinyl-covered walls, as well as all the other kinds of walls you have in your home. So in this chapter we're going to look into the best and quickest ways to clean the various surfaces in your home. In the next chapter, we'll get to the furniture.

WALLS

Walls get dirty in the same passive way that ceilings do: Grime and dust float through the air, land on them, and stick. But walls also get dirty in more active ways—when

61

toddlers try out their crayons, chocolate-bar eaters switch on lights, and exuberant chefs toss spaghetti. Unless you deal with the passive dirt buildup on walls, attempts to wipe up after your active family will result in a smeary mess or leave a streak of clean-wall color in sharp contrast to the rest of your wall.

Use your vacuum cleaner with a floor/wall brush to vacuum your walls whenever you clean the room. Remember to go behind pictures and mirrors with the small-brush attachment.

Use an all-purpose cleaner for cleaning washable walls. We recommend that you test the product by first washing an in-conspicuous place to make sure it does not harm your wall. Wash walls from the bottom to the top,

overlapping the cleaned areas to prevent streaks. We've found that you can keep water from running down your arm when you wash walls by making a bracelet from a sponge or washcloth held in place with a thick rubber band.

To remove transparent tape from a wall without marring the paint or wallpaper, use a warm iron. Through a protective cloth, press the tape with the iron to soften and loosen its adhesive backing.

Remove finger smudges while they are fresh. But do not scrub with excessive pressure, or use synthetic scouring pads or abrasive cleaners.

Brick

A wall made of brick requires little attention if you use your vacuum cleaner to remove loose dirt regularly. A solution of hot water and an all-purpose cleaner will clean accumulated dirt and stains from the surface. If the mortar between the bricks is especially dirty, add chlorine bleach to the cleaning solution. Wet the areas below a smoke stain before you wash it; this will prevent runoffs from staining the lower tiers of bricks.

Slight smoke stains above a fireplace opening are quickly removed with abrasive cleanser.

Scrub the cleanser into the moistened brick and then rinse with clear water, making sure no white residue remains. If spot-cleaning changes the color of the brick, you can even out the color by rubbing another brick of the same color over the discolored surface.

If the brick wall is especially dirty, use a commercial brick cleaner and a stiff-bristled brush. Rinse with clear, hot water, and wipe dry. **Caution:** Wear rubber gloves when using a strong solution, and keep it and other dangerous chemicals out of the reach of children.

Ceramic Tile

We recommend that you clean both glazed and unglazed ceramic tile regularly with an all-purpose cleaning solution or a spray tile-and-grout cleaner. **Caution:** Use rubber gloves to avoid skin contact, and don't breathe the mist when spraying the tile. Scrub dirt from the grout with a toothbrush or nailbrush, taking care not to scratch the tile. After cleaning, a clear-water rinse is recommended. Then buff with a soft, dry cloth to bring out the shine on glazed tile.

You can clean darkened grout with a solution of $1/4$ cup liquid chlorine bleach and 1 quart water. Scrub this cleaner into the grout with a toothbrush and rinse with clear water.

Grout can also be cleaned with a paste made from 3 parts baking soda and 1 part water. Apply this to the grout with a damp cloth, scrub with a toothbrush, and rinse with clear water.

CERAMIC-TILE CLEANER

Mix $1/2$ cup vinegar, 1 cup clear ammonia, $1/4$ cup baking soda, and 1 gallon warm water.

Caution: Wear rubber gloves to protect your hands, and work in a well-ventilated area. Applied to the wall with a sponge, this solution does a wonderful job of cutting grease and cleaning soil. Rinse with clear water.

Decorator Tile

Self-sticking decorator tiles, which are often vinyl-coated, are grease- and stain-resistant. A quick wipe with a sponge dipped in an all-purpose cleaning solution is usually all that is needed to keep them fresh and bright. You should try to avoid excessive moisture; it might seep between the seams and loosen the backing.

Metal Tile

We recommend that you wipe metal tile with a cloth dampened with an all-purpose cleaner and then buff with a soft, dry cloth to avoid streaking.

Mirror Tile

You clean all mirror tiles in the same way, whether they are clear, smoked, or have a design painted or etched on them.

We recommend that you use one of the homemade cleaners included here; they are as effective as commercial products and cost a lot less. Never use soap on mirror tile; it will streak and leave a film.

Painted

Most walls are painted with latex, which is easy to wash after it has "cured," or set for a period of time. The other kind of wall paint, alkyd, or oil-based, is more

MIRROR TILE CLEANERS

Mix $\frac{1}{3}$ cup clear ammonia in 1 gallon warm water. Apply with a sponge or squeegee or pour the solution into a spray container and spray it directly onto the mirror tiles.

Caution: Wear rubber gloves. Buff with a lint-free cloth, chamois, or paper towels. Vinegar may be substituted for ammonia.

- OR -

Mix 2 cups isopropyl rubbing alcohol (70 percent), 2 tablespoons liquid dish washing detergent, and 2 cups water. Stir the solution until thoroughly mixed, then pour it into a pump bottle, and spray it directly onto the mirror tiles. Buff with a lint-free cloth, chamois, or paper towels.

- OR -

Pour vinegar into a shallow bowl or pan, crumple a sheet of newspaper, dip it in the vinegar, and apply to the tile. Wipe the mirror tile several times with the same newspaper until it is almost dry, then shine the tile with a clean, soft cloth or dry newspaper.

durable than latex, but it is more difficult to apply. Both types of paint come in three finishes: flat, semigloss, and gloss.

We recommend that you clean painted walls with a commercial all-purpose cleaner or use the following recipe for a homemade painted-wall cleaner.

PAINTED-WALL CLEANER

Mix 1/2 cup vinegar, 1 cup clear ammonia, 1/4 cup baking soda, and 1 gallon warm water.

Caution: Wear rubber gloves, and work in a well-ventilated area when using this powerful solution. Apply the solution to the wall with a sponge and rinse with clear water. If your walls have a rough texture, use old nylon stockings or socks rather than a sponge because they won't tear and leave difficult-to-remove bits on the surface.

We have found that you can lift crayon marks off a painted wall by rubbing them carefully with a cloth or sponge dampened with mineral spirits or lighter fluid. Remove any shine by sponging it lightly with hot water.

Papered

Wallpaper is not washable. We recommend that you clean it only with commercial products, following the manufacturer's instructions for the best results. But we've found some simple, quick ways to clean up smears, spots, and writing on the wall between major cleaning.

- General soil comes off when a piece of rye bread is wadded up and used like an eraser.

- Smudges, fingerprints, and pencil marks can be removed from wallpaper by very gently rubbing the spots with an art gum eraser.

- To clean a grease spot, blot it with paper toweling and sprinkle cornstarch on the stain. After the cornstarch absorbs the grease, rub it off gently and vacuum.

- You can also place a white blotter over a grease spot and press it with a moderately hot iron. The blotter will soak up the grease. Repeat as required.

- To remove crayon from wallpaper, rub carefully with a dry soap-filled, fine-grade steel-wool pad. Or use a wad of white paper towels moistened with dry-cleaning solvent to delicately sponge the surface. Carefully blot and lift in small areas to prevent the solvent from spreading and discoloring the wallpaper.

Vinyl

If your wall coverings are made of vinyl, rather than paper, they're washable. Some manufacturers caution against using ammonia-based cleaners, so be sure to check the instructions for cleaning your vinyl wall covering or test the cleaning product you plan to use on your wall in an inconspicuous area.

CLEANER FOR VINYL WALL COVERINGS

Mix ½ cup vinegar with 1 quart water and gently apply the solution to the wall with a sponge.

Caution: Wear rubber gloves. Don't use too much moisture; it could seep under the seams and loosen the backing.

You can also use a "dry detergent" to clean a vinyl wall covering. Mix ¼ cup dishwashing liquid with 1 cup warm water in a bowl and beat the mixture to a stiff foam with an eggbeater. Working in a small area, dip a sponge into the foam and apply it to the wall to loosen dirt. Rinse the detergent with a sponge that has been dipped in clear water and squeezed dry.

Wood Paneling

Wood paneling has many different finishes, all of which should be cleaned in their own way. Paneling that was left natural or stained with a water-based stain and not sealed should only be cleaned with your vacuum cleaner. If your paneling has an oil finish, you can clean it with a commercial oil-based product or our home-made cleaner, but avoid any cleaning product that contains wax. If your paneling has a waxed finish, use only wax-based cleaners.

OIL FINISH

This make-it-yourself polish restores the beauty of wood paneling that has an oil finish. Pour equal parts turpentine and boiled linseed oil into a jar, tighten the lid, and shake the liquid to blend it thoroughly. **Caution:** Wear rubber gloves. Pour a small amount of the mixture onto a soft cloth and rub up and down the paneling, following the grain of the wood. The wood will appear oily, but within an hour the polish will be completely absorbed, leaving a soft sheen on your paneling.

Using your vacuum cleaner with the wall-brush attachment is the best way to clean loose dirt from all kinds of wood paneling. Never use water to clean wood. If you use a spray or aerosol cleaner/polish, follow the manufacturer's instructions carefully.

We've found that if you need to remove white water marks from wood paneling, you can rub mayonnaise into them. Wipe off the mayonnaise 12 hours later. The marks will have vanished.

WOODWORK

Woodwork is constantly assaulted with the same kind of dirt and grime that hits walls. Most woodwork is painted, stained, or left natural with an oil or varnish finish. All woodwork should be vacuumed regularly. Don't forget the tops of doorjambs, window frames, cornices, and ledges as well as baseboards.

We recommend that you keep a small container of matching paint or stain handy to touch up nicks and scratches on woodwork.

When you wash door and window frames, work from the bottom up, using an all-purpose cleaner on painted surfaces to remove smudges and fingerprints. Clean stained and natural woodwork with a wood cleaner/polish. Do not use water or water-based cleaners on stained or natural woodwork except for light touch-ups that you buff dry quickly. Spray the cleaner onto a cloth instead of directly onto the woodwork to prevent staining adjoining surfaces.

Many commercial oil and wax finishes are available. For best results, always follow the manufacturer's instructions.

FIREPLACES

A fireplace needs regular care and cleaning to assure its safety and efficiency. Creosote, a tarlike, flammable substance that builds up in the chimney and flue, must be removed to eliminate a potential fire hazard.

We suggest that you give your fireplace and its accessories routine cleanings throughout the wood-burning season; then you won't end up in the spring with an accumulation of soot, ashes, and creosote. Use your vacuum cleaner frequently to prevent dust and soot from building up on the hearth. But do not vacuum until all the embers have been extinguished for at least 12 hours.

Burn only seasoned, well-dried wood to minimize dangerous creosote buildup. Inspect the firebox, flue, and chimney yearly for creosote accumulation.

Do not use water to drown a fire; it will make a paste of the ashes that is difficult to remove. We recommend that you keep a fire extinguisher near the fireplace at all times.

Never use an abrasive cleanser inside the fireplace. Many leave a flammable residue, and they can wear away firebrick.

Andirons and Brass or Brass-Plated Tools

There are many commercially available products that can restore brass fireplace tools to their original beauty with a little time and effort. If you choose to use one, be sure to follow the manufacturer's instructions for the best results.

You can also clean andirons by dipping fine-grade (OOO) steel wool in cooking oil and rubbing gently. **Caution:** Wear rubber gloves to protect your hands. Apply polish to bring up the shine.

Chimney and Flue

Your fireplace chimney and flue must be cleaned properly at least every two years to assure a safe fire. But for the most efficient use of your fireplace, we suggest that you have it professionally cleaned once a year.

Firebox

The firebox is the part of the fireplace that contains the fire; it is commonly constructed of either metal sheeting or firebrick. Since the heat of the fire keeps the firebox clean (in much the same way a self-cleaning oven works), very little upkeep is required.

Gently scrub the walls of the firebox opening with a stiff-bristled brush (not a wire brush) to the height of the lintel (the steel brace that supports the masonry above the fireplace opening). Be gentle with firebrick because it crumbles easily. Be careful not to bend any edges

on a metal firebox where it joins the flue. Bent edges leave openings to the wall studs where fire could spread.

If your fireplace does not have an ash pit, shovel the bulk of the ashes into a trash bag. Then use your vacuum cleaner to remove the remaining lightweight ashes.

Fire Screen

Most fire screens are made of black-painted metal, but if your screen is brass plated, clean it as you would other brass objects.

If your brass-plated fireplace screen is coated with lacquer to protect its shine and this coating is cracked or peeling, you can clean it quickly with a solution of baking soda and boiling water (1 cup soda to 2 gallons water). Let the screen stand in the solution until it cools, then peel off the lacquer. You can either have the screen relacquered or clean and polish it.

You can also clean brass-plated fire screens by dipping fine-grade (OOO) steel wool in cooking oil and rubbing gently. **Caution:** Wear rubber gloves.

FIRE-SCREEN CLEANER

Mix 1/2 cup vinegar and 1 gallon warm water. Add 1 teaspoon ammonia.

Caution: Wear rubber gloves to protect your hands. Dip a cloth into the solution and wipe down both sides of the screen. Rinse with a cloth dipped in clear, warm water.

Glass Enclosure

Glass enclosures for fireplaces defeat their purpose if you can't see through them. The best way

CLEANER FOR GLASS FIREPLACE ENCLOSURES

Remove smoke stains with a solution of 1/2 cup vinegar in 1 gallon warm water. Add 1 tablespoon clear ammonia. Either spray this mixture on the glass or wipe it on with a cloth.

Caution: Wear rubber gloves. Rinse with clear, warm water and dry with a clean cloth.

to care for tempered, heat-resistant, glass is to keep it clean. After every second fire, remove the residue of soot from the glass.

If soot has baked on your glass fireplace enclosure, scrape the glass very carefully with a glass scraper. Avoid scratching the surface by taking your time and using a sharp blade.

Grate and Cast-Iron Tools

If you burn green wood, your fireplace grate can accumulate

a buildup of creosote or sap. If you always burn seasoned wood, you will probably never have to clean the grate.

We recommend that you remove creosote or sap that is not baked on the grate before you use the fireplace again. Take the grate outside and hose it down. If it is too cold to work outside, don't put off cleaning the grate; find a place to do this messy job inside. Sprinkle an abrasive cleanser on the grate; scrub with a stiff-bristled brush or use a steel-wool soap pad. No precautions need to be taken, but we recommend that you wear rubber gloves to protect your hands from abrasion.

If sap and creosote have baked onto your fireplace grate, the only way to remove the baked-on residues is with commercial oven cleaner. Work outdoors, wear rubber gloves, and observe all the manufacturer's suggested safety precautions. Allow the cleaner to sit overnight.

Unpainted iron surfaces, such as fireplace tools, that are not continuously exposed to the heat of the fire can rust. We suggest that you protect iron fireplace tools with liquid wax and buff them to bring up highlights.

Mantel and Hearth

Warming the room is usually a secondary occupation for most fireplaces; their primary function is to look good. A mantel gives you a place to put Aunt Sarah's heirloom clock, something to arrange the living room furniture around, and somewhere to lean when you need to have a formal picture taken. A blackened mantel and a dusty hearth won't fill the bill; your fireplace is a showpiece and should look like one. But keeping up appearances does not require daily drudgery if you follow our hints.

The trim surrounding a fireplace is usually made from masonry tile or wood. Brick, marble, and ceramic tile are also used.

Brick

You can quickly remove smoke stains from above a fireplace opening by using an abrasive cleanser. Scrub the powder into the moistened brick surface and then rinse well with clear water to make sure no white residue remains.

If brick is especially dirty, use a commercial brick cleaner and a stiff-bristled brush. Rinse with clear hot water and wipe dry.

Caution: Wear rubber gloves when using any strong solution, and be careful to keep it and other dangerous chemicals out of the reach of children.

Ceramic Tile

Both glazed and unglazed ceramic tile are used for mantels and hearths. Unglazed tile should be treated periodically with a sealer to keep its slightly porous surface from becoming stained. Glazed ceramic tile is virtually stainproof, but that isn't true of the grout that holds the tiles in place.

We recommend that you use a toothbrush or nailbrush to clean grout. Do not use harsh abrasive cleaners on stained grout; they might scratch the glaze on the ceramic tile.

Many aerosol-foam and spray tile-and-grout cleaners are

available. Always follow the manufacturer's instructions, then rinse with clear water and buff dry to finish the job. **Caution:** Wear rubber gloves to avoid skin contact with these powerful cleaners, and take care not to breathe the mist from spray cleaners.

CERAMIC-TILE CLEANER

Mix ½ cup vinegar, 1 cup clear ammonia, ¼ cup baking soda, and 1 gallon warm water.

Caution: Wear rubber gloves, and work in a well-ventilated area when using this powerful solution. Apply the solution to the mantel and hearth with a sponge and rinse with clear water. Wipe dry to prevent water spots.

Marble

Remove dust from your marble mantel with your vacuum cleaner. Then wipe with a damp sponge to remove light soil.

Abrasive or caustic cleaners will scratch marble. Oil polishes and soft waxes may discolor it. Many commercial cleaners are available, but borax rubbed into the surface with a moistened cloth will also clean marble. Rinse with warm water and buff dry with a soft cloth. This technique also brightens light-colored marble.

Masonry Tile

Masonry tile is very easy to care for. We recommend that you sprinkle dry baking soda onto the tile. Rub it with a soft-bristled brush to absorb stains and clean the tile. Use your vacuum cleaner to remove the dry powder.

Wood, Oiled or Waxed Natural Finish

Many commercial oil and wax finishes for wood are available. For the best results, follow the manufacturer's instructions.

Never apply wax or furniture polish over an oil finish.

Oil Finish

This make-it-yourself polish is one of the best products for restoring the beauty of mantels that have an oil finish. Pour equal parts turpentine and boiled linseed oil into a jar, tighten the lid, and shake the solution to blend it thoroughly. **Caution:** Wear rubber gloves. Pour a small amount of the mixture onto a soft cloth and rub the wood, following the grain. The wood will appear oily, but within an hour the polish will be completely absorbed, leaving a lovely soft sheen.

Wood, Painted

Mantels are usually painted with oil-based paints that are very easy to clean. First, use your vacuum cleaner to remove loose dirt. If your mantel has carved decorative elements, you may want to blow dirt from the carving by putting the hose in the blower end of your vacuum cleaner.

After you have removed all of the dust from the mantel, mix 2 tablespoons dishwashing detergent in 1 gallon warm water. Wipe it on with a cloth or sponge. Don't let any excess run off; it can stain surrounding surfaces. We recommend that you clean from the bottom up to avoid streaking.

RADIATORS, HEAT VENTS, AND RETURNS

Radiators, baseboard heating units, portable heaters, registers, and heat-distributing devices in the fireplace acquire dust from the air currents created by their heat. Unless you clean your heating outlets, they'll recirculate all that dirt onto your walls, draperies, and home furnishings. But when you clean them, you remove the dirt they have collected, quickly cutting down on dirt buildup in your home.

The best way to clean all kinds of heating units is to vacuum them with your vacuum cleaner. We suggest that you make it a habit to vacuum heating units whenever you vacuum the floor. Use a crevice tool to get into hard-to-reach places. For tight spots, such as between the fins of radiators, use the blower end of the vacuum and blow the dust out onto wet newspaper.

If you have forced-air heat, remove the grids covering the vents and returns, and vacuum their backs. Also, clean inside the duct as far as the hose of your vacuum cleaner will reach.

Wash the surfaces of radiators and baseboard units with an all-purpose cleaner when they begin to look grimy.

RADIATOR CLEANER

After thoroughly vacuuming the radiator to remove dust, clean the unit with a solution made from $1/2$ cup vinegar, 1 cup ammonia, $1/4$ cup baking soda, and 1 gallon hot water.

Caution: Wear rubber gloves, and work in a well-ventilated area when you use this powerful solution. Place newspapers and/or drop cloths under the radiator to protect the floor from moisture, and apply the solution with a sponge or cloth. Use a long-handled brush to clean the fins of radiators; a ruler draped with cloth will also work. Rinse with clear water.

WINDOWS

We suggest that you plan to wash your windows twice a year, usually in the spring and in the fall. If you get everyone in the household involved in window washing, you can probably finish the task on a Saturday morning.

Put some of your crew to work inside and others outside. Tell those who are at work in the house to use vertical strokes; those working on the outside should use horizontal strokes. With this method, you can quickly track down streaks.

We recommend that you use a squeegee on a long handle or a sponge/squeegee combination to prevent streaks on large windows. An old windshield-wiper blade makes a good squeegee.

WINDOW CLEANERS

Pour vinegar into a shallow bowl or pan, crumple a sheet of newspaper, dip it in the vinegar, and apply to the window. Wipe the glass several times with the same newspaper until the window is almost dry, then shine the glass with a clean, soft cloth or dry newspaper.

- OR -

Mix 2 cups isopropyl rubbing alcohol (70 percent), 2 tablespoons liquid dish washing detergent, and 2 cups water. Stir the solution until thoroughly mixed and then pour it into a spray bottle. The alcohol keeps the cleaner from freezing on windowpanes in cold weather.

- OR -

To remove built-up cooking grease or soot from windows, use a solution of 2 cups kerosene and 1 gallon warm water. Rub the mixture on the glass with a soft cloth and wipe the panes dry with clean paper towels.

Caution: Wear rubber gloves, and do not use this solution near an open flame because kerosene is flammable. This cleaner protects windows; water will bead on them in the same way it does on a waxed car.

Wash windows from the top down to prevent drips on sections you've already cleaned. Use a soft toothbrush or cotton swab to clean corners.

Soap will leave smudges on windowpanes, and abrasive cleansers or steel wool will scratch the glass. Window cleaners themselves pose a threat to woodwork. If the cleaner is allowed to drip on the windowsill, it can harm the paint or varnish.

We've found that if you wash windows on a hot or sunny day, the glass is likely to streak.

WINDOW COVERINGS

When you shut the shades to block the view or draw the drapes to hide the windows you didn't have time to wash, you end up looking at smudgy shades or dusty drapes. When light filters through your miniblinds or shutters, eventually the slats appear to be flocked with gray fluff. Then it's time to do something about your window coverings. As with all the other dirt catchers in your home, regular use of your vacuum cleaner will keep your curtains and blinds from disappearing in a cloud of dust. When more than dust is obscuring your drapes and shutters, we also know what to do.

Blinds

The best way to clean blinds is to vacuum them regularly with the small-brush attachment of your vacuum cleaner. Close adjustable slats when vacuuming so that you reach more of their surface.

You can remove finger marks with a damp sponge. But when blinds require a thorough cleaning, immerse them in water. Wash them outdoors by hanging them on the clothesline for scrubbing or in the bathtub. Natural wood blinds with decorative yarn tapes should not be immersed, but plastic, metal, and painted wood blinds can be cleaned in this way.

Pour a low-sudsing, all-purpose cleaner into a bathtub filled with warm water, or for outdoor cleaning mix a solution of 1/2 cup cleaner in 1 gallon warm water and apply with a brush. If you wear cotton gloves when you wash blinds, you can use your fingers to rub the slats. Rinse the blinds with clean water; allow them to drip-dry either on the clothesline or on the shower-curtain rod, placing

towels underneath them to catch drips. Rehang the blinds on the window when the dripping has stopped; stretch the tapes or cords to full length to prevent shrinking. Leave the slats in the open position until the blinds are completely dry.

Curtains

Carefully read the care label attached to new curtains, and follow the manufacturer's instructions for cleaning. Using the upholstery attachment on your vacuum cleaner, regularly go over curtain panels for quick cleaning. Vacuuming is almost all the cleaning that fiberglass curtains ever need.

We recommend that you vacuum curtains to remove excess dust before washing. Also disconnect curtain rings and clips (unless they are permanently attached) to prepare your curtains for washing.

Fiberglass curtains should be washed and never dry-cleaned. You must wear rubber gloves when hand washing them to protect your hands from glass filaments. Thoroughly rinse the washing machine after washing fiberglass to ensure that no fine glass fragments remain in the tub.

Handle cotton curtains gently if they have been hanging in a sunny window; sunlight may have weakened the fabric. Machine wash sheers, open weave, and other delicate fabrics in a mesh bag or hand wash so that the fabric does not stretch or tear.

Tumble or drip-dry curtains, according to their fabric. Use curtain stretchers for drying lace or net curtains, and iron curtains

that need to be pressed before they are completely dry.

Draperies

Draperies are often lined and are usually made of fabrics that are much heavier than those used for curtains. It is usually best to dry-clean draperies, but some drapery fabric is washable; check the care label.

Dust draperies with the upholstery attachment on your vacuum cleaner. Also vacuum drapes before you wash them or send them out to be cleaned. Don't forget to dust the tops of the drapes, the valances, and the drapery hardware. Occasionally air draperies on a clothesline on a breezy day to refresh them between cleanings.

Remove all hooks and pins unless they are permanently

attached before washing or dry-cleaning. If you plan to wash your draperies, test a corner of the fabric in a bowl of warm water and detergent to see if it bleeds. Use only the gentle cycle to wash draperies.

Shades

Light-diffusing or opaque shades usually are made of fabrics that are washable, and some shades have a protective vinyl coating that makes them very easy to clean. Other shades are not washable and must be dry-cleaned.

Vacuum shades regularly, using the small-brush attachment of your vacuum cleaner. Lower the shades completely before vacuuming to clean the full length. Don't forget the tops of the shades and the valances.

Remove finger marks with a damp sponge or a quick spray of all-purpose cleaner. To thoroughly clean the shades, remove them from the window and spread them out on a flat surface. Test a corner of the shade with a detergent solution to see if the color bleeds.

Make a mild soapsuds solution using a liquid dishwashing detergent, and apply it to a rolled-out shade with a sponge. Rinse with a clean sponge dipped in clear water, and allow the shade to dry before rerolling.

Some spots on nonwashable shades can be removed with an art gum eraser. Use it as though you were erasing a pencil mark. You can also clean grease spots on shades that can't be washed by thoroughly rubbing the surface with a rough, absorbent cloth dipped in cornmeal. The secret of this treatment is that the abrasiveness of the cloth and the absorbency of the cornmeal work together to pick up soil and grease. Terry cloth is good for this job, but an old sweatshirt turned inside out is even better. Dry kitchen flour can be substituted for cornmeal.

Shutters

We recommend that you vacuum all shutters regularly with the small-brush attachment of your vacuum cleaner. Wipe them occasionally with a damp sponge to remove smudges and fingerprints.

For painted shutters, the best care is probably the least, since some polishes and waxes can damage the color and/or decoration. Use warm, soapy water with a damp cloth to wash painted shutters; wash each louver separately on both sides. If you feel you must wax, use a hard paste wax only once a year.

Shutters finished with wax, varnish, or lacquer can be cleaned with commercial aerosol polishing/waxing products. Choose a product that is appropriate for the high-gloss or satin finish of your shutters, but do not spray any cleaner directly onto the shutters because it can seep into the dowels and clog the louvers.

CHAPTER 4
Inside Your Living Areas

If your home is like most, much of your furniture probably does all kinds of things it wasn't intended to do. The upholstered chair by the front door is a catchall for schoolbooks and jackets. The dining table doubles as a sewing table, desk, or computer center. And many of us practically live in bed, watching TV, snacking, reading, or just recovering from the day at work. Grime builds up on the chair, lint sticks to the dining table, and cracker crumbs work their way into the mattress.

We've found that you can maintain (or restore) the good looks of most furniture with the proper care. You can use (or misuse) your furniture the way you want, and still seat your great aunt in that upholstered chair, serve company dinner on the dining table, and roll over in your sleep without crunching crumbs. In this chapter, you'll find time-tested techniques for cleaning, polishing, and protecting the many different kinds of furniture and the treasured objects you have in your home.

BOOKS

If you arrange books at the front of shelves, air will be able to circulate around them to prevent mustiness. You should also protect books from direct sunlight, which will fade the bindings and cause them to deteriorate.

The best way to clean books is to vacuum them with the small-brush attachment on your vacuum cleaner. Tilt each book back and then forward, one at a time, on the shelf so you can remove the dust from the book's binding and edges.

To keep imitation-leather book bindings looking as good as new, wipe the covers with a mild detergent solution, and then treat them with a light coating of petroleum jelly or vinyl dressing. Leather-bound books should be treated periodically with lightweight oil so that the leather won't dry out and crack.

To remove grease stains from books, rub the affected areas with soft white-bread crumbs. Badly soiled paper edges of books can be cleaned with an art gum eraser. Hold the book firmly by the covers so that you won't accidentally damage the pages if the book falls open.

If a book is damp, sprinkle the pages with cornstarch until the moisture has been absorbed, then vacuum the powder.

DECORATIVE OBJECTS

The decorative objects you've collected and cherish add visual interest to your home and sometimes become treasured family heirlooms. They'll also need to be cleaned from time to time. Most of your things can be safely cared for at home, especially if frequent dusting has kept dirt from building up on their surfaces.

Alabaster

Alabaster looks like marble and is made into vases, statues, lamp bases, and other ornamental objects. Although it comes in several colors and sometimes has a dark streak or band of color, the best-quality alabaster is pure white and translucent. It is fine-grained but soft enough to be scratched with a fingernail. Alabaster is easily broken, soiled, and weathered, and must be handled with care.

Dust alabaster frequently with a soft, untreated cloth or the small-brush attachment of your vacuum cleaner. We recommend that you gently blow dust away from intricate carving with the vacuum's blower.

ALABASTER CLEANER

Clean alabaster with borax; it is mild enough not to scratch the surface. Dip a moistened cloth into a small amount of dry borax and rub it on the alabaster. Rinse with warm water and buff dry with a soft cloth.

An oil polish or soft wax will probably discolor alabaster, and abrasive or caustic cleaners will scratch it. Alabaster can be cleaned with commercial products that clean marble. **Caution:** Work in a well-ventilated area to avoid breathing fumes from these products; do not smoke while using them or work near an open flame because some marble-cleaning products are flammable.

Brass

There are many brass polishes on the market. If you run out of the polish you usually use, we suggest you try one of the following solutions:

Brass Cleaners

- Make a paste from 1 tablespoon salt, 1 tablespoon flour, and 1 tablespoon vinegar. Apply the paste with a soft cloth and rub.

- Dip a cut lemon in salt and rub it on the brass. Wash the object in warm soapsuds and buff it dry to bring up the shine.

You can strip cracked and peeling lacquer from coated brass and brass-plated objects with a solution of baking soda and boiling water (1 cup soda to 2 gallons water). Let the article stand in the solution until it cools, then peel off the lacquer.

You can either have the piece relacquered or clean and polish it yourself.

Copper

You can clean and polish copper with one of the many commercial copper-cleaning products that are on the market. But if you don't have the cleaner you usually use on hand, try one of these methods:

Copper Cleaners

- Make a paste of 1 tablespoon salt, 1 tablespoon flour, and 1 tablespoon vinegar. Rub it over the surface, then wash the copper object in hot, soapy water. Rinse and buff for a shiny finish.

- Mix 2 tablespoons vinegar and 1 tablespoon salt to make a copper cleaner. Wash, rinse, and dry the item after using this treatment.

- A cut lemon dipped in salt will also clean copper.

Gold

Gold has a brilliant luster that resists corrosion and tarnish. Gold is very soft and is usually combined with other metals to add hardness. The number of carats describes the purity of the gold: 24 carats is pure gold; 18, 14, and 10 carats have lesser amounts of gold.

GOLD CLEANER

Mix 1 teaspoon baking soda with enough water to form a paste. Rub the paste onto the gold object with a soft cloth, rinse, and buff dry with a chamois.

Jade

Jade is used to make lamp bases, vases, carved ornaments, and jewelry. It is hard, heavy, and fine-grained. The color of jade ranges from white to dark green, with occasional tints of brown, mauve, blue, yellow, red, gray, or black.

Because jade is hard and not porous, very little care is required. Dust it regularly, and buff it with a soft cloth or chamois when it begins to look dull. If a jade piece becomes soiled or sticky, wipe it with a damp cloth and buff it with a dry cloth.

Marble

Marble is used to make many things including tabletops, floors, countertops, fireplace facings, window and door sills, and statuary. It comes in a variety of colors and has either a shiny or a matte finish.

Vacuum marble surfaces regularly using the small-brush attachment of your vacuum cleaner. Then wipe them with a damp sponge to remove light soil and buff to dry. Do not use abrasive or caustic cleaner on marble; it will mar the surface. We suggest that you not use oil polish or soft wax, it may discolor the marble.

Commercial polishes, some of which are flammable, are available for cleaning marble. Read and follow the manufacturer's directions.

MARBLE CLEANER

Using borax is an effective, inexpensive way to clean marble. It is mild enough not to scratch the surface. Dip a moistened cloth into a small amount of dry borax and rub it on the marble. Rinse with warm water and buff with a soft cloth. This technique brightens light-colored marble.

Pewter

Pewter can be cleaned with the outer leaves from a head of cabbage. Rub a leaf over the surface and then buff it with a soft cloth.

Porcelain

Porcelain and other types of clay are used to make vases, lamp bases, candlesticks, and figurines that depict everything from Elvis to Plymouth Rock.

Dust porcelain regularly with the small-brush attachment of your vacuum cleaner or a soft cloth.

When a porcelain object becomes dirty, wash it in mild soapsuds, using warm water. Hot water can cause the glaze to crack. Pad the bottom of the sink with a towel and wrap another towel around the faucet to prevent breaking a delicate object in the sink. Never use abrasives or steel-wool pads on porcelain and do not wash it in the dishwasher.

SILVER POLISH

Make a paste of 3 parts baking soda to 1 part water. Using a soft cloth, rub the paste gently on the silver. Tarnish will disappear rapidly. After rinsing, buff the silver with a soft cloth to bring up the shine.

Silver

When properly cared for, silver just gets better looking as it grows older. With many polishings and much handling, sterling silver will develop a satin patina. This blending of many tiny scratches, known as a "butler's finish," gives the silver an overall luster.

SILVER POLISH

Place tarnished silver in a glass dish, add a piece of aluminum foil, and cover with 1 quart hot water mixed with 1 tablespoon baking soda. A reaction between the foil and the silver will remove any tarnish. Don't use this process on silver objects with raised designs; you will lose the dark accents of the pattern.

FURNITURE

The furniture in your home can be made of just about anything, from stone to straw and plaster to plastic. All furniture lasts longer and looks better if you clean it regularly. Use your vacuum cleaner to remove dust and dirt, and when necessary, clean and polish your furniture using the techniques we suggest.

You'll need to know what your furniture is made of in order to select the proper cleaning and polishing methods. Before you clean a piece of furniture for the first time, read the product label carefully to learn safety precautions and whether the cleaner you plan to use suits the surface. If you do not know what your furniture is made of, test your cleaning product in an inconspicuous place before cleaning the entire piece.

Metal

Metal furniture often requires no special care. Vacuum it regularly and wipe it with an all-purpose cleaning solution on a dampened sponge or rag.

PLASTIC-FURNITURE CLEANER

Using baking soda is the cheapest way to rid plastic furniture of stains. Just sprinkle the soda on the stain, rub it with a damp cloth or sponge, and rinse with clear water.

Plastic

Vacuum plastic furniture regularly with your vacuum cleaner's small-brush attachment. Wipe it occasionally with a sponge dipped in an all-purpose cleaning solution, and buff it dry to prevent streaks. We recommend that you remove stubborn spots with liquid detergent applied directly to the spot; then rub, rinse well, and buff dry. An abrasive cleanser or steel-wool pad will mar plastic and plastic laminate. Ammonia and alcohol-based products can cloud the surface. Apply appliance wax or light furniture wax to brighten dull plastic surfaces. This treatment will also protect plastic from scratches.

Upholstery

Treat spots and spills immediately, before they become stains, taking care to choose the appropriate spot remover for the kind of padding in upholstered pieces. Don't use solvent-based spot removers on cushions filled with foam rubber; solvents can deteriorate foam rubber.

Acid stains on upholstery should be treated especially quickly. Dilute them immediately with baking soda and water or with club soda. The same solution will also keep vomit stains from setting.

Fabric

When vacuuming or spot cleaning fail to make your upholstered furniture look fresh, then it's time to shampoo or deep-clean the fabric.

UPHOLSTERY SHAMPOO

Mix ¼ cup dishwashing liquid with 1 cup warm water and whip the solution with an eggbeater. Apply the foam to the upholstery, a small section at a time, with a soft-bristled brush. Shake off any excess water. Rinse the upholstery by gently rubbing the fabric with a moist, clean cloth; rinse the cloth as necessary.

Most furniture upholstered in fabric can be shampooed safely at home; the exception to this is fabric marked "dry-clean only." But it is safe to spot clean this kind of fabric with a solvent-based cleaner.

Many commercial fabric shampoos are available. Always read and follow the manufacturer's instructions.

Leather

Leather must be cleaned with pure soap products (no detergents) and benefits from occasional applications of conditioner to restore moisture and bring up the sheen.

> ## LEATHER-UPHOLSTERY SHAMPOO
>
> A sudsy solution of soap flakes and warm water is a good way to clean leather upholstery. Apply the suds only, scrubbing gently with a soft-bristled brush; wipe clean with a damp sponge.

Vinyl

Vinyl upholstery is sometimes difficult to distinguish from real leather. It can be cleaned in the same way as leather or with a commercial cleaner developed especially for cleaning vinyl. Never use oil; it will harden the upholstery.

Vinyl upholstery is very durable, but it can easily be punctured or cut. This kind of damage is difficult to repair, so do not allow sharp objects to come in contact with this upholstery material. You must also be careful when you vacuum not to scratch the vinyl with sharp-edged attachments.

> ## VINYL-UPHOLSTERY SHAMPOO
>
> The best way to clean vinyl upholstery is with baking soda on a damp cloth, followed by a light washing with dishwashing liquid.

Wood

Oiled

Oiled-wood surfaces have a warm, soft glow and require only an occasional application of furniture oil to keep them looking nice. Be careful never to wax an oil finish.

Wet drinking glasses leave white spots or rings on oil-finished furniture. You can rub them with toothpaste on a damp cloth. (Try this on other surface stains as well.) Or rub the white spots with a mild abrasive and oil. Appropriate abrasives are ashes, salt, soda, or pumice; suitable oils are olive oil, petroleum jelly, cooking oil, or lemon-oil furniture polish.

OIL FINISH

Pour equal parts turpentine and boiled linseed oil into a jar, tighten the lid, and shake the liquid to blend it thoroughly.

Caution: Wear rubber gloves. Pour a small amount of the mixture onto a soft cloth and rub the surface of the furniture, following the grain of the wood. The wood will appear oily, but within an hour the polish will be completely absorbed, leaving a lovely, soft sheen.

Painted

For painted-wood furniture, the best care is probably the least, since some polishes and waxes can damage the color and decoration.

Vacuum the furniture regularly, using the small-brush attachment. Wipe the piece with a damp sponge to remove smudges and fingerprints. If you feel you must wax, use a hard paste wax no more than once a year.

Polished

Polished-wood furniture is finished with varnish, lacquer, or wax. Any commercial aerosol polishing/waxing product will clean and polish wood surfaces quickly. Choose a product that is appropriate for the high-gloss or satin finish of your furniture.

Paste wax gives a harder, longer-lasting finish than spray or liquid polish and is recommended for antiques. Although paste wax takes a bit of "elbow grease," the beautiful results are worth the effort.

CLEANER FOR POLISHED WOOD

Wipe polished wood furniture with a cloth dipped in cold black tea. Buff to dry.

If you wear cotton gloves while you wax furniture, you will not leave fingerprints. Or you can sprinkle cornstarch over the surface of recently polished furniture and rub it to a high gloss. Cornstarch absorbs excess oil or wax and leaves a glistening surface that is free of fingerprints.

There are several ways to remove white spots, such as those left by wet drinking glasses. You can rub them with toothpaste on a damp cloth, with paste furniture polish, or with a mild abrasive and oil. Appropriate abrasives are ashes, salt, soda, or pumice; suitable oils are olive oil, petroleum jelly, cooking oil, or lemon-oil furniture polish.

Specialty

Specialty-wood furniture is made of wicker, rattan, bamboo, cane, and rush. This kind of furniture usually has a natural finish, but some pieces may have a varnish or shellac coating.

Vacuum specialty-wood furniture regularly with the small-brush attachment of your vacuum cleaner.

With the exception of rush chair seats that are damaged by moisture, occasionally wet down specialty woods outdoors with a garden hose or in the shower to restore moisture to the fibers to keep them soft. Wetting cane seats tightens them; spray the unvarnished side with water and allow it to air-dry.

If specialty-wood furniture is very dirty, clean it with an all-purpose cleaner. Rinse well and allow it to dry thoroughly before using it again.

LAMP SHADES

Since many lamp shades direct a beam light onto their collected cobwebs and dust, they'll need to be cleaned more frequently than less-obvious dirt collectors. Lamp shades are made of many different materials. Some are washable and some are not; keep all the care information from the manufacturer so you know the proper cleaning procedure for your lamp shade.

You can easily remove dust and cobwebs from lamp shades with the small-brush attachment of your vacuum cleaner.

Wash silk, nylon, and rayon shades only if they are sewn onto their frame. Dry-clean shades that are glued to their frames. Remove spots from nonwashable fabric shades with spot remover.

We recommend that you use your bathtub or a large laundry sink to wash lamp shades. Make a sudsy warm-water solution with liquid dishwashing detergent. Dip the shade in and out of the solution, making sure that the shade is completely covered, and then rinse it in lukewarm water, following the same dipping procedure. Rinse until the water is clear. Take the shade outside and swing it vigorously in a circle to get rid of excess moisture, and then dry it in the sun or with an electric fan or hair dryer.

If your lamp shade is washable but has glued-on trim that prevents you from immersing it in water, use the following method for cleaning:

LAMP-SHADE CLEANER

Mix ¼ cup dishwashing liquid with 1 cup warm water and whip the mixture with an eggbeater until it makes a stiff foam. Apply the foam to the shade with a sponge, being careful not to wet the trim. Rinse by going over the shade with a clean cloth wrung out in clear water. Allow the shade to dry.

Plastic and fiberglass shades need only be wiped occasionally with a damp cloth to remove soil.

We suggest that you clean lamp shades that are made from parchment or wallpaper with commercial products especially formulated to clean these surfaces. Follow manufacturer's instructions.

MIRRORS

If you want the mirrors in your home to reflect well on you, you'll have to keep them spotless. This won't take much time, since mirrors are easy to clean, and when mirrors sparkle, the whole room looks brighter.

If you use a liquid glass cleaner on your mirror, don't allow moisture to collect along the edges or in the corners of the mirror frame. This can cause the glue holding the frame to loosen or the silver backing on the glass to peel, crack, or discolor. We recommend that you keep glass cleaner away from the mirror frame by holding a blotter or towel against the frame while you are cleaning the mirror.

MIRROR CLEANERS

Mix ⅓ cup clear ammonia in 1 gallon warm water. Apply with a sponge/squeegee or pour it into a pump bottle and spray sparingly onto the mirror. Buff with a lint-free cloth, chamois, or paper towels. Vinegar may be substituted for ammonia.

- OR -

Mix 2 cups isopropyl rubbing alcohol (70 percent), 2 tablespoons liquid dish washing detergent, and 2 cups water. Stir until the solution is thoroughly mixed and then pour it into a pump bottle. Spray the mixture sparingly on the mirror, and buff it with a lint-free cloth or paper towels.

- OR -

Pour vinegar into a shallow bowl or pan, crumple a sheet of newspaper, dip it in the vinegar, and apply to the mirror. Wipe it several times with the same newspaper until the mirror is almost dry, then shine it with a clean, soft cloth or dry newspaper.

PIANOS

A piano is a valuable instrument, made with expert craftsmanship, and a major investment for most households. Your piano should be treated with respect and care. Whether or not your piano is being played regularly, we recommend that you have it tuned frequently by a licensed piano tuner. Have this done approximately four times during the first year you own a new piano, semiannually for an older instrument, and whenever your piano is moved from one location to another.

Pianos should be protected from changes of temperature, drafts, and humidity. Direct sunlight can also damage a piano. For these reasons, an upright piano should be placed against an inside wall of your home and a grand piano should sit away from windows and heating units.

Dust the piano case regularly with a soft cloth and vacuum the interior occasionally with the small-brush attachment and crevice tool of your vacuum cleaner. Keeping the top of a grand piano closed when the instrument is not being played protects it from potentially damaging dust buildup. Also cover the keyboard when it is not in use if the keys are plastic; ivory keys need to be exposed to light to prevent them from yellowing.

Use a nonsilicone furniture polish or wax on the case of a piano that has a varnish or lacquer finish. A piano that has a high-gloss, polyester epoxy finish can be cleaned with a damp cloth or chamois and buffed dry; it should never be waxed or rubbed with furniture polish.

Dust the keyboard regularly with a soft cloth treated with a spray-on dusting aid. Wrap the cloth around the eraser end of a pencil to get between the keys. Some smudges on the keys can be eliminated by rubbing them with the eraser. To remove stubborn stains from ivory or plastic keys use a damp cloth dipped in baking soda, being careful not to let the soda fall between the keys. Wipe the keys with a soft, clean cloth.

PICTURES

Paintings, whether oil, acrylic, or watercolor, and photographs, whether framed behind glass or dry-mounted, require a minimum amount of care.

If the painting or photograph is damaged, we recommend that you have it repaired or cleaned professionally.

If the frame or glass over a picture is damaged, you may be able to make the repairs yourself or simply reframe your picture.

Vacuum the painting, frame, and glass regularly, using the small-brush attachment of your vacuum cleaner.

When you clean the glass over a painting, be careful not to allow any moisture to get behind the glass. Also, do not spray furniture polish directly on picture frames. Spray it on a cloth and then carefully apply the polish to the frame, making sure that it does not get on the painting or under the glass.

To make a tarnished gilt frame gleam again, wipe it with a rag dampened with turpentine.

SLIPCOVERS

Slipcovers usually are washable. Refer to the manufacturer's care instructions or the fabric-care label for cleaning information.

We recommend that you use your vacuum cleaner to remove lint and dust from slipcovers before washing them. Mend any ripped seams, close all zippers and fasteners, and pretreat heavy soil and spots before washing.

Machine wash slipcovers whenever possible. Hand washing is suitable only for small pieces. Select the appropriate water temperature for the fabric, but never use hot water if there is any possibility of shrinking or fading.

Machine-dry the slipcover until it is slightly damp, not completely dry. Press pleats or ruffles if necessary before refitting the slipcover on the furniture. We recommend that you put a slipcover back on the furniture while it is still damp for a smooth fit.

BEDDING

When sheets and pillowcases are soiled, you can just toss them in the washing machine along with the rest of the wash. But other kinds of bedding require special care.

The key to successful cleaning is to do it before the soil is heavy and to know the fabrics involved in order to use the right cleaning procedures. We suggest that you keep a file of manufacturers' care labels and refer to them when cleaning is necessary.

Bedspreads

Many bedspreads are washable. Before you wash your bedspread, we suggest that you dip a corner of it in the detergent solution you plan to use to check for colorfastness. If the color bleeds, have your bedspread dry cleaned.

If it is safe to wash your bedspread, we advise you to wash it before it becomes heavily soiled. Treat spots and stains with a spray prewash product or liquid detergent. Use a large commercial washing machine for oversized bedspreads. An overcrowded washer won't clean very well. Dry bedspreads across several clotheslines or in a large commercial dryer.

Blankets

Blankets are made of many different fibers and blends, but most of them are washable by hand or machine. Always check the care label and follow the manufacturer's instructions.

Before you wash a blanket, mend or replace bindings and treat spots and stains. Use a large commercial washer to wash large blankets. Fill the washer with water and put in the detergent so it can completely dissolve before you add the blanket. Use a gentle (delicate) wash cycle; long periods of agitation will mat blanket fibers. Avoid overcrowding the machine. A fabric softener will increase a blanket's fluffiness and reduce static electricity.

Use your vacuum cleaner to remove dust and lint from blankets. We suggest that you also air blankets on a clothesline periodically to refresh them.

Electric blankets should always be hand or machine washed, never dry-cleaned. Both cleaning solvents and mothproofing can damage the wiring in an electric blanket.

Comforters and Quilts

Down-Filled

The down filling in comforters and quilts is held in place by tufts of yarn or by stitched-through patterns.

Most down-filled comforters and quilts are washable, but some older ones are too fragile to be cleaned at home. Follow the manufacturer's care instructions if they are available.

Test older comforters and quilts for colorfastness by wetting an inconspicuous spot with the detergent solution you plan to use and blotting the area with a white blotter.

If comforters or quilts are in good condition, machine wash and dry them. Use cold wash water and rinse water and all-purpose detergent. Fragile down comforters and quilts should be hand washed in the bathtub or a deep laundry tub.

Drape the wet comforter or quilt over several clotheslines to allow excess moisture to drip out; reposition it periodically. If the comforter or quilt is strong enough to be dried in a clothes dryer, preheat the dryer to a low temperature and include a pair of clean, dry sneakers to help fluff the down. The dryer can also be set on air dry (no heat) to dry the quilt.

Wool-, Cotton-, and Synthetic-Filled

Padded bed coverings may be filled with wool, cotton batting, or polyester fiber. The filling is held in place by tufts of yarn or by stitched-through patterns. Most cotton- or polyester-filled comforters and quilts are washable, but older quilts may be too delicate to withstand washing. Some newer wool-filled or wool-covered comforters and quilts can be washed at home; others should be dry-cleaned.

Follow the manufacturer's care instructions if they are available. Test old quilts and comforters for colorfastness before attempting to wash them by wetting a small area with the detergent solution and blotting it with a white blotter. Clean patchwork quilts with the method that is appropriate for the most delicate fabric in the quilt. Never wash silk- or velvet-covered quilts and comforters.

For small- to medium-size quilts and comforters, use your home washing machine. For large quilts, use a commercial washer. Let quilts and comforters soak in the machine for about 10 minutes before starting them through a short, gentle (delicate) washing cycle.

Hand wash and line-dry old or fragile quilts and all quilts with cotton batting. Machine washing is too harsh and can cause cotton batting to bunch up. Use a bathtub or deep laundry tub, and allow the soap or detergent to dissolve in the wash water before adding the quilt.

Mattresses and Box Springs

Mattresses are usually made with foam or springs and casings, while futon mattresses are often stuffed with cotton. Regardless of what a mattress is made from, all benefit from routine care.

Vacuum mattresses and box springs, and turn the mattress over and around end-to-end to ensure even wear. Use an upholstery attachment on your vacuum cleaner, and work carefully around any buttons on your mattress. Remove dust and blanket fluff from the edges of the box spring with your vacuum brush attachment.

We recommend covering mattresses with quilted or rubberized pads that can be quickly washed when they become soiled. Remove spots and stains promptly, but do not allow

the mattress to become excessively wet when you spot clean it. Let the mattress completely dry before making the bed.

Pillows

Know the pillow's filling—down, feathers, foam, polyester, or kapok—so that you can use the appropriate cleaning method. For polyester-filled pillows, read the care-instruction tags; some polyester-filled pillows are washable, but some are not.

Kapok is the silky covering of seeds from the ceiba tree. Pillows with this stuffing need frequent airing but cannot be washed.

We recommend that you protect your pillows with a zip-on cotton or polyester cover, which you can wash regularly. Refresh pillows by airing them near an open window or hanging them on a clothesline outside.

Down and Feather

Fluff down and feather pillows when you make your bed to get rid of accumulated dust and to redistribute the filling. Before you wash a feather or down pillow, make sure it has no holes or ripped seams.

Machine or hand wash feather and down pillows in cool water with cold-water, light-duty detergent. Wash two pillows at a time or add a couple of bath towels to balance the load. If the fabric is worn or the pillow is heavily stuffed, wash the feathers and ticking separately. Secure the feathers in a large muslin bag and stitch the opening closed.

Dry down and feather pillows in the dryer on the low-heat setting. Including a pair of clean, dry tennis shoes in the dryer will help distribute the down as it dries.

Foam

Hand wash and line-dry foam pillows. Change the hanging position hourly to dry the filling evenly. Never put a foam pillow in the dryer.

Polyester-Filled

Machine or hand wash polyester-filled pillows in warm water with an all-purpose detergent. A front-loading tumble washer rather than a top-loading machine works best for polyester pillows. Dry the pillows in the dryer on a moderate heat setting.

CHAPTER 5
Kitchens

We want our kitchens to be light, sparkling (or cozy) multiuse family centers, complete with computers and couches, TVs and miniature vegetable patches. Gathering the family around the hearth or the induction cooktop is a terrific idea. But don't forget that in the middle of all the activity and nice furniture, there's still a kitchen, where you're going to be spilling milk and burning toast. Cooking is a messy task. The only way to deal with the mess in the kitchen is to control it with quick, daily cleanups.

In most households, there are cooks and there are eaters. Use this division of labor to everyone's advantage for regular kitchen maintenance. Cooks should blot spills when they happen and put dirty cooking utensils into the sink or dishwasher. But after dinner, the cleanup crew (previously known as the eaters) takes over from the cooks. They'll vacuum crumbs with a handheld vacuum, do the dishes, wipe the countertops and appliances, clean the sink, and take out the garbage. Keeping the kitchen fairly clean beats having to spend regular long stretches of time cleaning it.

COUNTERTOPS

Kitchen countertops have to be ready for anything—a smack from a floury handful of bread dough, a slice from a paring knife that goes off course, or a slosh of grape juice intent on staining the surface. Acrylic, ceramic tile, cultured marble, marble, plastic laminate, and wood countertops can take this kind of abuse if we make it up to them with regular, gentle cleaning and care.

Acrylic

You have to go out of your way to harm an acrylic countertop. A very hot pan will leave a permanent burn mark on the surface, but scouring powder or steel wool will remove most stains and scratches. For routine cleaning, use mildly abrasive liquid or powdered cleansers, applied directly onto the wet surface to dissolve dirt. Rinse well and buff dry with a soft cloth.

ACRYLIC CLEANER

Mix ½ cup vinegar, 1 cup ammonia, ¼ cup baking soda in 1 gallon warm water.

Caution: Wear rubber gloves and work in a well-ventilated area when using this powerful solution. Apply it to the acrylic countertop with a sponge, rinse with clear water, and buff dry.

Ceramic Tile

Both glazed and unglazed ceramic tile are used for kitchen counter-tops. Unlike many other surfaces, ceramic-tile countertops can take the heat; you don't have to fumble around searching for a trivet whenever you need to find a safe place to set a hot pot. Ceramic tile itself is extremely durable, but the grout between the tiles is soft, porous, and prone to cracks.

CERAMIC-TILE CLEANER

Mix ½ cup vinegar, 1 cup clear ammonia, ¼ cup baking soda, and 1 gallon warm water.

Caution: Wear rubber gloves and work in a well-ventilated area when using this powerful solution. Apply the solution to the countertop with a sponge and rinse with clear water. Wipe dry to prevent water spots. Mix a fresh batch of cleaner for each cleaning session.

Use a toothbrush or nailbrush to scrub grout clean. To remove

GROUT CLEANER

Put 3 cups baking soda in a medium-size bowl and add 1 cup warm water.

Caution: Wear rubber gloves. Mix to form a smooth paste; scrub it into the grout with a toothbrush and rinse thoroughly after cleaning. Mix a fresh batch of cleaner for each cleaning session.

mildew and other stains, dip the brush in laundry bleach. When you clean grout, don't use harsh abrasive cleaners, which might scratch the glaze on ceramic tile. Many aerosol-foam and spray tile-and-grout cleaners are available. Always follow the manufacturer's instructions, and rinse with clear water to finish the job. **Caution:** Wear rubber gloves to avoid skin contact with these powerful cleaners, and take care not to breathe the mist from spray cleaners.

Cultured Marble

Cultured marble is an acrylic material that resembles real marble, but it's easier to care for because it is less porous and does not have to be sealed.

CULTURED-MARBLE CLEANER

Mix ½ cup vinegar, 1 cup ammonia, ¼ cup baking soda in 1 gallon warm water.

Caution: Wear rubber gloves and work in a well-ventilated area when using this powerful solution. Apply it to the cultured marble with a sponge, rinse with clear water, and buff dry.

Avoid abrasive cleaners and steel-wool soap pads; they will scratch the surface. Mildly abrasive liquid or powdered cleansers should be applied directly to the wet surface to dissolve dirt and soap film. Rinse well and buff dry with a soft cloth.

Never place a hot pot directly on cultured marble because it will leave permanent burn mark.

Marble

Marble countertops are porous and susceptible to stains, but they are not affected by heat. Seal marble with a special stone sealer to reduce its porousness. Make sure to always wipe up wine, fruit juice, and other acid food spills immediately to prevent permanent etching to the surface.

Abrasive and caustic cleaners will mar the surface of marble, and oil polishes and soft waxes may discolor it. Many appropriate commercial cleaners are available, but borax rubbed into the surface with a moistened cloth will also clean marble. Rinse with warm water and buff dry with a soft cloth.

Plastic Laminate

Plastic-laminate countertops can be found in many kitchens. They're practically seamless, giving cooks a waterproof, smooth work surface that is easy to clean. Unfortunately, wetness is not the only difficulty we must expect our kitchen countertops to overcome: There are also hot cooking pots, sharp knives, and red-wine vinegar, to name a few. Plastic laminate burns, scratches, and stains fairly easily, so you'll have to be considerate of your countertops to keep them looking good. Regular applications of appliance wax or light furniture wax will help plastic-laminate surfaces to resist stains and scratching. Never use abrasive cleansers or steel wool on laminate countertops, and always use a cutting board.

PLASTIC-LAMINATE CLEANER

Using baking soda is the cheapest way to rid countertops of stains.

Caution: Wear rubber gloves when working with this cleaner. Sprinkle the soda on the stain, rub it in with a damp cloth or sponge, and rinse with clear water.

For general cleaning, a two-sided scrubbing pad with fiber on one side and a sponge on the other works particularly well. The fiber side, moistened slightly with water, is just abrasive enough to loosen greasy smears and other soil. Turning the scrubber over, use the sponge side to wipe the surface damp-dry. When a spot or stain persists, apply a polishing cleanser with a wet sponge. Then rinse and damp-dry the countertop.

Wood

Butcher-block and other wood countertops require more care than you might expect, if you don't want them to look like they belong in the back room of a butcher shop. You can restore a wood countertop that has been scratched and stained by sanding it and applying a wood-preservative product, but that's a lot of work. You'll save time in the long run by preserving your wood countertop's good looks. Always use a cutting board on a wood countertop, just as you would with any other surface. Wipe up stains and keep your wood countertops as dry as you possibly can. Periodically, rub oil into wood countertops to protect them from moisture. Use boiled linseed oil or salad oil and follow the procedure described here.

WOOD-COUNTERTOP CLEANER

Baking soda cleans and deodorizes wood surfaces. Mix $1/2$ cup cup baking soda in 1 quart warm water.

Caution: Wear rubber gloves. Rub the paste into the wood countertop, using a synthetic scouring pad. Rinse well with clear water and pat dry to remove excess moisture. When completely dry, restore the finish by using boiled linseed oil or salad oil, rubbed in with a fine-grade steel-wool pad. Treat the countertop with two coats of oil, applied 24 hours apart, and blot up the excess oil after each application.

Remove stains with a solution of $1/4$ cup chlorine bleach in 1 quart warm water. Rinse, dry, and coat with oil.

To get rid of odors, rub the surface with a slice of lemon.

DRAINS

We all know that cooking grease combined with bits of food jams kitchen-sink drains, and we know that prevention is the best cure for the problem. But most of us will have blocked kitchen drains anyway.

As soon as a drain begins to run slowly, treat it; don't wait until no water drains out. If you suspect that the problem is a grease deposit, dissolve it by pouring boiling water or boiling water and baking soda down the drain.

If this treatment does not open the drain and if either a dishwasher or a garbage disposal is connected to it, call a plumber immediately. If no appliances utilize the drain, you can attempt to open it with a plumber's helper.

If plunging fails to unclog the drain, use a chemical drain cleaner. These products must be handled with care because they are caustic and harmful to skin and eyes. Use them in a well-ventilated area and follow the manufacturer's instructions carefully.

Commercial drain openers are sold in granular, liquid, and pressurized forms. Granular products utilize lye to do their work, liquid drain openers use lye and other chemicals, and pressurized products work by chlorofluorocarbon propellants and pressure. Before you use a granular drain opener, you must remove standing water from the sink; this is not necessary for liquids. If the first type of chemical drain opener you use does not work, do not use a different drain opener unless the initial cleaner has been flushed away totally. Never use a plunger or a pressurized drain opener after using a chemical cleaner; either one may cause dangerous chemicals to splash back onto you. Also, be sure to tell your plumber what you have put into the drain before he or she starts to work. The combination of ammonia and other household cleaners with drain cleaners produces hazardous gases.

HARDWARE

Get in the habit of wiping faucets and taps when you swab the counters after meals. This will prevent water spots and give your kitchen a sparkling look with very little effort on your part. Clean hardware when you clean the sink, using the same cleaning product and method. Rinse well and buff with a dry cloth. Wash greasy drain baskets in the dishwasher.

LARGE APPLIANCES

Large appliances are basically big, enamel-coated metal boxes that clean up with the swipe of a wet cloth. With the exception of rangetops that have at least four depressions to trap and hold spilled food, the outsides of appliances present no cleaning problems.

You give them a once-over when you do your countertops, and that's that. Inside large appliances, there's another story.

If you keep up appearances by regularly wiping sticky fingerprints off the refrigerator door and gummy drips off the front of the dishwasher, you can put off cleaning the messes that lurk within your large appliances until you have time to deal with them thoroughly. When you do find the time to tackle the interiors, we're here to help with time-tested hints to speed you through your work.

Dishwashers

Baking soda cleans your dishwasher inside and out. Dip a damp cloth in soda and use it to clean smudges and fingerprints from the exterior; the same method will also remove stains from the liner. Use a synthetic scouring pad to clean stubborn soil.

Use a spray glass cleaner to polish chromium trim. Commercial kitchen-appliance waxes will leave a protective wax coating on your dishwasher, but be careful not to get wax on the plastic parts.

If your dishwasher has a butcher-block top, clean it by saturating a cloth or fine-grade (OOO) steel-wool pad with vegetable oil, rub it into the wood, and allow the oil to soak overnight. Wipe up any excess oil the next day.

If your dishwasher's interior retains odors, sprinkle 3 tablespoons baking soda in the bottom of the machine and allow it to sit overnight. The odors will be washed away with the baking soda during the next wash cycle. To prevent the liner from retaining odors, occasionally leave the dishwasher door open to air.

Here's a quick way to remove mineral deposits from your dishwasher. Use this method only for dishwashers with porcelain interiors. It cannot be used on dishwashers with plastic interiors. Place a glass bowl containing ¾ cup bleach on the lower rack. Load the dishwasher with glasses and dinnerware only and run it through the wash and rinse cycles. Then put 1 cup vinegar in the bowl and run the dishwasher through another complete cycle.

Freezers

Freezers require little care other than wiping off smudges and fingerprints and defrosting (if you have a manual defrost model).

Defrost the freezer when the frost gets to be ½-inch thick. Turn off the freezer controls and remove all the food. Put the food in an ice chest, wrap it in layers of newspaper, or store it tightly packed in your refrigerator. Open the door of the freezer and allow the ice to melt partially. When it is the consistency of slush, scrape the ice away with a wooden or plastic scraper. You can speed the melting process by setting shallow pans of hot water on the freezer shelves. Do not put food back into the freezer until you have wiped off any condensation that develops

---

FREEZER CLEANING

Make a solution of 1 tablespoon baking soda and 1 quart warm water and wash the interior of the freezer.

Caution: Wear rubber gloves. Dry the interior with a soft cloth after washing and before turning the freezer back on. The baking soda not only cleans but also deodorizes the freezer.

Dip a damp cloth in baking soda and rub the exterior of the freezer to clean dirt and smudges. Rinse well and wipe dry with a soft cloth.

and the freezer has been running for at least half an hour.

Whenever you defrost your freezer, clean dust from behind the grill at the bottom of the freezer with your vacuum cleaner.

Place a box of baking soda in the freezer every other month to control freezer odors.

Microwave Oven

If you keep a microwave oven clean, you'll never have to "clean" it. Just wipe the exterior when you do the kitchen countertops, and wipe the interior after each use.

A synthetic scouring pad will remove stubborn soil. Use a mild dishwashing detergent, baking soda, or glass cleaner. Wash the glass tray in the sink or the dishwasher when it is soiled. Never use a commercial oven cleaner in a microwave oven.

Range Hoods

Some range hoods are vented to the outside and remove grease, steam, and cooking odors from the kitchen. But other hoods do not have outside vents and rely on replaceable charcoal filters to clean smoke and odors from the air. Both vented and nonvented hoods have fans to draw air and smoke from the cooking area, and both need to be cleaned to keep them free from grease buildup and working effectively.

Wipe the exterior and interior of the range hood. Use a solution of hot water, dishwashing detergent, and ammonia to cut the grease; wear rubber gloves. Remove the filter cover and wash it in soapy, hot water. Allow it to dry completely before replacing. Wipe the blades of the fan with an ammonia solution.

Clean metal mesh filters when they are dirty, and replace the filters on nonvented range hoods every six to nine months or as often as the manufacturer recommends. Washing charcoal filters will reduce their effectiveness.

Ranges

The best way to care for your range is to clean it continually, never allowing spilled food or grease spatters to become baked on. If you wipe up spills as soon as the stove is cool, they will not bake onto the surface and cleaning will stay simple.

Ceramic Cooktops

The ceramic cooktop is a glass cooktop with electric heating elements under the glass. While smooth tops may appear to be easy to clean, special care must be taken to avoid damaging or discoloring the ceramic surface.

Wait until the top cools to wipe up spills; never use a wet sponge or cloth on a hot panel. Don't set soiled pots or pans on the surface; they can mar it permanently. Abrasive cleaning products will scratch the surface, discoloring it and making it difficult to keep clean.

The best way to clean a ceramic cooktop is to sprinkle a nonabrasive cleanser or baking soda over the surface and rub with a synthetic scouring pad or sponge. Rinse well with clear water and buff dry with a soft cloth for a clean finish.

Gas and Electric Stovetops and Range Exteriors

The exteriors of most gas and electric ranges are baked-on porcelain enamel, the trim is usually chromed steel or brushed aluminum, and the control knobs are plastic.

Wipe the surface around the heating elements after each use. Use a synthetic scouring pad for stubborn soil. Harsh abrasives or steel wool will damage the stove's enamel finish.

Wash reflector bowls, or drip pans, and grids in warm soapsuds whenever food or grease is spilled on them. Clean reflector bowls will help your stove to cook more efficiently; blackened and dull reflector bowls absorb heat rather than reflecting it back up to the cooking pot. Whenever you remove the bowls from the stovetop to wash them, use your vacuum-cleaner hose to draw out crumbs and other particles that collect beneath them. Many stovetops can be raised for access to this area.

Gas burners should be washed occasionally. Clear the holes with a fine wire or a pipe cleaner. Don't use a toothpick; it could break off and clog a hole. To prevent rust, quickly dry the gas burners in a warm oven after they have been washed.

Electric heating elements are self-cleaning and should never be submerged in water. If you need to clean an element, first turn off the power to your electric range at the service panel.

Remove all the control knobs when you clean the exterior of the range to make the job easier. Soak the knobs in sudsy, warm water and dry them with a soft towel before putting them back in place.

Commercial appliance-cleaning products will not only clean and shine the surface of your range but also will leave a protective wax coating.

Ovens

There are many strong cleaning products designed to clean traditional ovens. **Caution:** Most oven cleaners are dangerous when they come in contact with your skin or eyes. Wear rubber gloves and protect your eyes while cleaning. Don't breathe the spray mist or the fumes. Avoid dripping oven cleaner onto any surfaces other than those it is intended to clean. Always read and follow the manufacturer's instructions when you use a commercial oven cleaner.

OVEN CLEANER

Pour 1 cup ammonia in a glass or ceramic bowl, place it in a cold oven, and allow it to sit in the closed oven overnight. The next morning, pour the ammonia into a pail of warm water and use this solution and a sponge to wipe away the loosened soil.

Caution: Wear rubber gloves whenever you work with an ammonia solution. The fumes are strong at first, but they soon dissipate.

When you clean a traditional oven, use strips of aluminum foil to protect the heating elements, oven wiring, and thermostat from commercial oven cleaners.

Many ranges are equipped with self-cleaning or continuous-cleaning ovens. A self-cleaning oven uses a pyrolytic, or high heat, system to incinerate oven grime, creating a powdery ash. A continuous-cleaning, or catalytic, system eliminates small spatters through the porous porcelain-enamel finish on the oven liner, which absorbs and spreads soil to promote cleaning at normal temperature settings. Large spills must be wiped up; they will burn and may permanently stain the oven surface. Dust continuous-cleaning ovens frequently and self-cleaning ovens after the cleaning cycle, using the small-brush attachment of your vacuum cleaner to remove dried food particles and/or ash.

Carefully follow the manufacturer's instructions when using the cleaning cycle of a self-cleaning oven, and follow the manufacturer's recommendations for caring for a continuous-cleaning oven. Neither kind of oven should be cleaned with commercial oven cleaners. A continuous-cleaning oven should

never be scrubbed with abrasives or powdered cleansers; these products will damage the surface.

Refrigerators

A frost-free refrigerator should be cleaned when it's dirty. Clean a manual-defrost refrigerator when you defrost the freezer compartment.

Wash the drip pan whenever you defrost and/or clean your refrigerator.

Defrost the freezer section of your refrigerator when the frost gets to be ½-inch thick. Turn off the freezer controls and remove all the food. Put the food in an ice chest or wrap it in layers of newspaper. Remove all shelves, bins, racks, and trays and wash them in a mild soapsuds solution. Dry thoroughly.

To speed defrosting, prop open the door of the freezer compartment. If your refrigerator is a manual-defrost model, placing shallow pans of hot water on the shelves will melt frost buildup quickly. When the ice is the consistency of slush, scrape it away with a wooden or plastic scraper. Never use sharp tools to scrape frost and ice from the freezer.

Do not put food back into the freezer until you have wiped off any condensation that develops and the freezer has been running for at least a half hour.

Wipe the interior of the refrigerator to prevent puddles from remaining in the bottom when you replace the bins.

Vacuum dust from the area behind the bottom grill of your refrigerator at least twice a year. Clean the condenser coils with your vacuum cleaner's crevice tool about once a month.

Control refrigerator odors with a box of baking soda placed at the back of a shelf. Replace the box several times a year. Also, place a box of soda in the freezer if odors are a problem there.

Do not wash ice trays in a detergent solution; this can remove the special nonstick coating that some of them have.

Commercial kitchen appliance wax will remove smudges and dirt and leave a protective wax coating on the exterior of the refrigerator, but baking soda will also clean and shine your refrigerator. Rub the exterior with a damp cloth dipped in baking soda, rinse well, and wipe dry.

Trash Compactors

Follow the manufacturer's cleaning instructions for the interior of your trash compactor. Clean it when necessary, watching out for small glass particles that may be left from the trash.

Generally, the bags made especially for a particular trash compactor will give you the best results. Remember that no compactor is designed to handle wet garbage. Empty your trash compactor frequently and use a deodorant spray to discourage bad odors.

Routinely wipe the exterior of your trash compactor to remove smudges and fingerprints. Use a commercial kitchen-appliance wax or baking soda to polish it.

SMALL APPLIANCES

The little machines that line up along our kitchen countertops or park themselves in our appliance garages save us time and effort when we cook. But they sometimes seem to use up the time they've saved us in the amount of time they take to clean. Food sloshes out of blenders and spins out of food processors. Blades and cutters hide food in their intricate designs and can cut our fingers when we try to clean them. Even though most small appliances are designed to be easy to clean, they still have to be cleaned. We'll show you quick and easy ways to do this without endangering yourself.

Blenders and Food Processors

Read and follow the manufacturer's cleaning instructions. Most plastic work bowls and blender jars can be washed in your dishwasher; some cannot. Some blades are dulled by repeated exposure to dishwasher detergents; some are not.

Wipe the bases of food-preparation appliances after each use, and you will rarely have to scrub them. The blender jar is almost fun to clean; fill it with a warm detergent solution and run the blender for about 15 seconds at high speed. Rinse well and dry. To retain the sharpness of the blades, do not wash the blender's assembly in the dishwasher.

Wash the food-processor work bowl, cover, pusher, blade, and discs in warm, soapy water or in the dishwasher. Because the blade is razor sharp, to be safe, carefully wash it by hand.

A glass cleaner is excellent for cleaning stainless-steel blender bases and trim. Simply spray it on and buff dry immediately with a soft cloth. An all-purpose cleaner or a solution of baking soda and water cleans plastic blender and food-processor bases.

Coffee Makers

Drip coffee makers are easy to clean; they require a new filter; washing the pot, lid, and basket in a detergent solution; and a quick wipe of the base with a damp cloth.

Percolators need thorough, occasional cleanings to get rid of oil build-up in the stem, basket, and interior walls that can affect the taste of the coffee.

Allow a heated percolator to cool before cleaning. We recommend that you use a synthetic scouring pad, never harsh abrasives or steel wool, to remove stubborn soil from percolator parts. If the surface becomes scratched, oil and other coffee residues will accumulate in the scratches.

Wash all percolator parts in a warm detergent solution after each use. If your percolator is not immersible, wipe the exterior with a damp cloth and buff dry. Clean the spout and tubes of a percolator with a percolator brush and a warm dishwashing-detergent solution.

Commercial products formulated to clean percolators are very effective, but we've found that the following method for cleaning percolators works equally well: With the stem and basket in place, fill the percolator completely full with cold water and add 6 tablespoons baking soda. Plug in the machine and allow the percolator to run through its complete cycle. Wait for 15 minutes, unplug the machine, and empty the solution. Wash in a mild detergent, rinse, and dry.

Electric Can Openers

Your can opener needs light but regular care. Remember always to unplug a can opener before cleaning it, and do not immerse the case in water. Wipe the can opener after each use to remove food spills or drips. Use a sponge dampened in a warm soapsuds solution made from liquid dishwashing detergent. Buff dry.

Periodically, remove the cutting wheel and lid holder and soak them in hot, sudsy water. Scrub caked-on food with a toothbrush; rinse, dry, and replace the parts.

Garbage Disposers

Garbage disposers are self-cleaning, but they can get smelly, especially if you let food sit in them for any length of time.

To keep your disposer odorless and running smoothly, operate it with a full stream of running cold water. Flush the disposer for a few seconds with cold water after turning it off to ensure that all debris is washed away.

Always keep the following materials out of the disposer: metal, wood, glass, paper, or plastic objects; fibrous organic waste, such as artichoke leaves and corn husks; and caustic drain cleaners.

If an unpleasant odor begins to come from your disposer, eliminate it by tearing up citrus fruit peels and put them into the disposer. Grind them with a stream of cold running water and enjoy the fresh smell.

Another excellent method for clearing odors from your disposer is to sprinkle baking soda over several ice cubes and grind them in the disposer.

Toaster Ovens/Broilers

When the puddle of cheese from last night's nachos meets the crumbs from this morning's toast in the bottom of your toaster oven, you have a major mess, not to mention a fire hazard.

Cleaning your toaster oven/broiler right after you use it prevents a squalid buildup of food spatters and crumbs, which is likely to become a permanent condition because baked-on messes are very difficult to remove from toaster ovens. Wipe the exterior of the oven and the crumb tray regularly, and wipe the interior of the oven with a warm dishwashing solution after cooking greasy foods. A synthetic scouring pad will remove stubborn soil from the tray and racks. The plastic parts are best cleaned with a warm detergent solution; buff the surfaces dry to avoid water spots.

CLEANER FOR THE TOASTER-OVEN/BROILER

A toaster oven/broiler usually has a polished-metal surface. The fastest way to clean it is to dip a dry cloth in baking soda and rub it over the oven. For stubborn soil, moisten the cloth first and apply soda with a gentle scrubbing action.

Caution: Wear rubber gloves. Dust off any soda residue. The finish will be shiny and scratch free.

Clean a toaster oven only when it is cool and has been disconnected. Never immerse the oven in water, and don't use harsh abrasives, steel wool, or commercial oven cleaner to clean a toaster oven.

Toasters

Toasters are crumb catchers and smudge collectors; they need regular attention to keep them clean, shiny, and crumb free. Remember to unplug the toaster and let it cool before cleaning it. Wipe the exterior of the toaster regularly. Remove the crumb tray at the base of the toaster and shake out accumulated crumbs; wash the tray in warm soapsuds. If your toaster does not have a crumb tray, turn the toaster upside down and shake it over the sink or a large garbage can. Use a thin, soft-bristled brush to remove crumbs from the interior.

Never wash the inside of the toaster with water or immerse the whole unit. Metal utensils should not be used to clean the inside of the toaster. You can polish the exterior of your toaster with baking soda or flour, using the same method we use for toaster ovens/broilers.

KITCHENWARE

Cookware

When was the last time you saw your face reflected in the bottom of a skillet or reveled in the warm glow of a copper pot you had just shined? If you can't remember, you probably have much too much to do to worry about keeping your pots, pans, and cooking utensils looking like new. Unless they're on display, a reasonably clean cooking pot functions just about as well as a sparkling clean one does. The amount of shine on your cookware is totally up to you. In this section, we'll tell you how to put a shine on stainless steel when you want to, but we'll also show you how to care for your cast iron easily and quickly.

Basic care for all cookware starts with reading the manufacturer's care instructions. Wash all pots and pans thoroughly inside and out soon after use. An exception to this is your omelet pan. Clean seasoned omelet pans with a paper towel. If baked-on food necessitates washing the pan in soapsuds, dry it thoroughly over a warm burner and rub vegetable oil into the warm pan with a pad of folded paper towels.

Prevent heat stains on the outsides of pans by keeping gas flames low so that they cannot lick up the sides. Do not subject cookware to sudden temperature changes. Allow it to cool before washing or soaking.

We recommend that you clean scorched pans by bringing 1 teaspoon baking soda and 1 cup water to boil in the pan. Allow the pan to cool and wash it in soapy water. Substitute vinegar for baking soda to clean scorched aluminum pans.

Aluminum

The only way to protect aluminum cookware from discoloration is never to wash it in an automatic dishwasher or let it soak in soapy water for long periods of time. We recommend that you don't allow food to stand in aluminum cookware and don't use it to store food; food that is acid-based can discolor or pit the metal.

CLEANER FOR DISCOLORED ALUMINUM COOKWARE

To remove interior discoloration, fill the pan with water, add 1 tablespoon cream of tartar or 1 tablespoon lemon juice per quart of water, and simmer until the discoloration is gone. Complete the cleaning process by scouring the pan with a steel-wool soap pad.

Caution: Wear rubber gloves.

Use a steel-wool soap pad to remove burned-on food from cast-aluminum cookware. Liquid nonabrasive bathroom cleanser or a paste of baking soda and water used with a synthetic scouring pad will polish both cast and sheet aluminum.

Cast Iron

Cast-iron cookware has a tendency to rust if it is not kept properly seasoned. Many new cast-iron cooking utensils come from the factory already sealed, but some will have to be seasoned before their first use.

If your cast iron pan requires seasoning, we recommend that you do it in the traditional way: Scour your pot with a steel-wool soap pad, then wipe the inside with vegetable oil, place it in a warm oven for two hours, and wipe off the excess oil. To maintain your cookware's seasoning, repeat this procedure periodically and whenever rust spots appear.

Wash cast-iron cookware in hot, sudsy water, then dry it thoroughly and store it in a dry cupboard without its lid in place. Never wash cast-iron cookware in the dishwasher; it will remove the seasoning and cause rust.

Clay

You should always soak new clay cookware in water for about a half hour before using it for the first time. Soak both the top and the bottom, then scrub them well with a stiff-bristled brush to remove clay dust.

Line the cooker with parchment paper to prevent the porous surface from absorbing food stains and strong flavors. If your clay pot becomes stained or takes on pungent odors, fill the cooker with water, add 1 to 4 tablespoons baking soda, and let it stand overnight.

Never put a hot clay cooker on a cold surface; the cooker might crack. Wash clay cookware immediately after it cools to prevent food from drying and crusting, but never wash clay cookware in the dishwasher or scrub it with a steel-wool soap pad. Carefully dry the cooker before storing it to prevent mold. Storing clay cookware with its lid off will also discourage mold.

If mold spots appear on a clay cooker, brush the surface with a paste made of equal parts baking soda and water. Let stand 30 minutes, preferably in strong sunlight; brush the paste away, rinse well in clear water, and dry thoroughly in a well-ventilated location.

Copper

Copper darkens with use and exposure to air. If you prefer shiny copper, you can clean and polish it easily. Copper cookware is lined with other metals to prevent harmful chemical reactions with food. The lining is usually tin or stainless steel. If your copper pot has a tin lining, you must be careful not to scrape away the tin by stirring with sharp metal cooking utensils. You can have a copper pan retinned when the lining begins to wear thin, but this is an expensive procedure. We recommend that you use wood, nylon, or nonstick-coated spoons for stirring to prevent scratching the lining of copper cookware.

Some copper cookware comes with a protective lacquer coating that must be removed before the utensil is heated. Follow the manufacturer's instructions, or place the

COPPER POLISH

To clean a discolored copper pot, use a paste of 1 tablespoon salt, 1 tablespoon white vinegar, and 1 tablespoon flour.

Caution: Wear rubber gloves. Because the vinegar is acid, wash the pot in hot soapy water and rinse it. Then buff vigorously for shiny results. (You'll have the same success with a paste made of 2 tablespoons lemon juice and 1 tablespoon salt.)

utensil in a solution of 1 cup baking soda and 2 gallons boiling water, let it stand until the water is cool, peel off the lacquer, wash, rinse, and dry.

Protect copper pans from scorching by making sure there is always liquid or fat in the pan before it is placed on the heat. When melting butter, swirl it around in the bottom of the pan and up the sides. Lower the heat as soon as the contents of the pot reach the boiling point.

Commercial copper-cleaning products do a good job of cleaning and shining copper cookware if you follow the manufacturer's instructions.

Enamelware

We suggest that you let enamel cookware cool before washing. Rapid changes in temperature can crack the enamel coating. If necessary, soak a dirty pot to loosen cooked-on foods. Use a synthetic scouring pad, never abrasive cleansers or steel wool, to scrub stubborn soil. Enamelware can be washed safely in the dishwasher.

Dishwashing detergent will clean enamel cookware quickly. Encrusted food or stains can be removed with a liquid nonabrasive bathroom cleanser.

Glass and Ceramic-Glass

Most heat-resistant glass and ceramic-glass cookware is designed for oven use only, but some can be used on stovetops. Read the manufacturer's instructions carefully to make sure that you use your cookware appropriately. All glass and ceramic-glass cookware is dishwasher safe.

Glass cookware that is allowed to boil dry is likely to shatter. If a pot boils dry, the safest way for you to handle this potentially explosive situation is to turn off the heat and leave the pot where it is until it has cooled.

You can remove mineral deposits from a glass coffeepot or teapot by boiling full-strength cider vinegar in the container for 15 minutes.

Nonstick-Coated

Nonstick finishes or coatings are relatively thin and damage easily. We recommend that you use wood, nylon, or specially coated spoons and spatulas to prevent surface damage. Most nonstick-coated cookware can be safely washed in the dishwasher.

CLEANER FOR NONSTICK COOKWARE

When you want to remove stains from nonstick-coated cookware, mix 2 tablespoons baking soda with 1 cup water and $1/2$ cup liquid bleach. Boil the solution in the pan for several minutes until the stains disappear. After washing the pan, wipe the inner surface with cooking oil to season it.

Wash new pans before using them and lightly coat the inside with vegetable oil. Apply vegetable oil again after each washing in the dishwasher and after treating stains, following the procedure described above. Do not soak pans in soapy water; the coating can retain a soap flavor.

Stainless Steel

Stainless steel requires practically no special care. It is dishwasher safe, but if you wash it by hand, dry it promptly to prevent water spots.

Allowing a gas flame to lick up the sides of a pan or letting a pot boil over high heat for a long period of time will discolor stainless steel. Storing your cookware stacked with other pots may cause surface scratches.

STAINLESS-STEEL POLISH

Sprinkle baking soda on the wet surface of a pan and scrub the metal with a synthetic scouring pad.

Caution: Wear rubber gloves. After rinsing and drying, the pan will be as bright as new.

Many commercial products will shine stainless steel. We recommend that you follow the manufacturer's instructions for the best results.

DINNERWARE

Almost every meal you eat at home results in dirty dishes. That could be more than a thousand sinkfuls of dishes annually. Washing dishes is one of the few housecleaning tasks that is truly unavoidable; the trick is to get it done and out of the way as quickly as possible. Here are a few hints to help you do dishes without doing yourself in.

Of course, the best hint for making dishwashing easier is to use a dishwasher. If you have a dishwasher, carefully read the manufacturer's instructions for loading, correct water temperatures, and preferred dishwasher detergents.

We recommend that you remove food residues from dinnerware as quickly as possible. Scrape dishes with a rubber scraper or plastic brush to prevent scratches. Never scrape plates with knives or other sharp objects. Rinse out coffeecups and teacups before residues have a chance to stain the cups.

Use cool water to soak or wash dishes that have been used to serve eggs or cheese. Acid foods, such as tomatoes, vinegar, and wine, allowed to remain on glazed dinnerware can pit the surface.

To protect glass or china from chipping or breaking while you

are hand washing it, use a plastic dishpan or rubber sink mat. You can also pad the bottom of the sink with a towel. Avoid abrupt changes of temperature when you wash china.

Do not wash delicate, hand-painted, gold- or silver-trimmed, or antique dinnerware in the dishwasher. Metal-trimmed dinnerware should also not be soaked in soapy water for long periods of time; this will damage the trim.

High temperatures may also damage dishes. Do not warm plates in the oven unless they are heatproof. Do not rinse glazed dinnerware with very hot or boiling water; this may cause the glaze to craze, or develop minute cracks.

FLATWARE AND CUTLERY

Most of us wash the knives, forks, and spoons we use at mealtimes along with our other dishes. If we're organized and wash dishes by hand, the flatware is washed after the glasses and before the plates. But washing flatware doesn't complete the cleaning process; unless you eat with stainless steel, your flatware will need to be polished occasionally.

Cutlery can be cleaned in the same way as flatware, but observe the manufacturer's instructions to be sure that the cutlery is dishwasher safe. Here are some tips for cleaning and polishing flatware and cutlery.

Always wash pewter and gold-plated flatware by hand and buff dry to bring up the shine and prevent water spots.

Use silver often; it tarnishes less and grows more beautiful with use. Store silver and gold flatware in rolls, bags, or cases made with tarnish-resistant cloth.

Sterling silver and silver plate may be washed in the dishwasher, but they will need to be polished less often if they are washed by hand. Rinse salt and acid food off flatware as soon as possible to avoid stains.

Do not allow stainless-steel flatware to touch anything made of silver in the dishwasher. It will set up an electrolytic action that pits the stainless steel and leaves black spots on the silver.

Do not soak flatware or cutlery that has bone, ivory, or wood handles; and do not wash them in the dishwasher.

Wash flatware and cutlery with liquid dishwashing detergent. Fill the sink with hot water, add the detergent, and wash the flatware using a soft cloth or sponge to wipe away the soil. Never use an abrasive cleanser, steel-wool pad, or synthetic scouring pad. Avoid overcrowding the sink to prevent scratching your flatware. After it is clean, rinse with hot water, and buff with a soft towel to bring up the shine.

Flatware Polishes

Gold: Place 1 teaspoon baking soda in a small bowl; add enough water to make a paste. Using a soft cloth, rub the paste over the gold-plated flatware. Rinse and buff dry with a soft cloth or chamois.

Pewter: Save the outer leaves from a head of cabbage and use them to polish pewter flatware. Rub the leaf over the surface of the pewter, and then buff with a soft cloth.

Stainless Steel: Sprinkle baking soda on the wet surface and scrub with a soft cloth or sponge. Wipe with a damp cloth and buff with a soft, dry cloth.

Silver: Combine 3 parts baking soda with 1 part water to form a paste. Using a soft cloth, rub the paste gently on sterling-silver or silver-plated flatware. The tarnish should disappear rapidly. After rinsing, a quick buff with a soft cloth brings up the shine.

GLASSWARE

Most glassware can be safely washed in the dishwasher, but gilt- and silver-trimmed glass, delicate crystal, milk glass, and ornamental glass must be washed by hand. If you have soft water in your area, we recommend that you wash all glassware by hand because the combination of soft water and dishwasher detergent will etch and permanently dull glassware.

Before you wash glassware, cushion the bottom of the sink with a towel or rubber mat. Add vinegar to the wash water or rinse water for more sparkle; ammonia in the wash water will cut grease on glassware. Wash glasses first, before cutlery or dinnerware. Slowly slide stemware into the wash water, holding the glass by the base; if you push a glass into the water bottom first, it could crack. Remove dirt from crevices with a soft-bristled brush; remove stains by rubbing with a cut lemon or washing in a vinegar solution. Let glassware drip dry upside down, or polish with a soft, lint-free cloth.

Clean stained decanters by filling them with water and adding 1 cup ammonia or vinegar. Soak overnight. If this solution does not clean the decanter, use two packs of powdered denture cleaner dissolved in water.

FOOD-PREPARATION, SERVING UTENSILS, AND STORAGE

Most food-preparation, storage, and serving utensils are made of plastic, rubber, metal, or wood. Metal is the easiest to clean, since it can be washed, does not retain food odors, and does not deteriorate in water the way wood does. The other materials, while relatively simple to care for, do need special treatment.

Metal

Metal cooking utensils, such as pancake turners, potato mashers, and cooking forks, are usually made of aluminum or stainless steel. They can be cleaned in hot, soapy water or put through the dishwasher. Never soak metal utensils with glued-on handles; the adhesive will weaken.

Plastic and Rubber

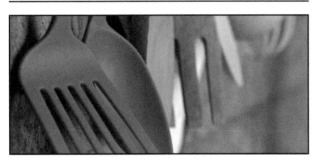

Plastic utensils and containers, such as orange-juice pitchers, covered storage bowls, and spatulas, and rubber food-preparation tools, such as scrapers, drain boards, and sink mats, are cared for in much the same way. We recommend that you don't expose plastic and rubber to high heat. Some plastics will melt and warp, and heat and sunlight can cause rubber products to crack.

Check the manufacturer's instructions to see if an item is dishwasher safe. Do not use solvents, harsh abrasives, or scouring pads to remove stains from plastic or rubber.

A thick paste made with equal parts baking soda and water is very effective for removing stubborn soil and stains from plastic and rubber utensils. It deodorizes as it cleans. Apply the paste to plastic with a sponge or soft cloth; a synthetic scouring pad can be used on rubber. **Caution:** Wear rubber gloves.

Another way to remove odor from a plastic container is to crumple a piece of newspaper into the container, secure the lid tightly, and leave it overnight. The paper will absorb the odor.

Wood

Wood food-preparation equipment, such as bowls, trays, rolling pins, spoons, salad utensils, and cutting boards, needs special care to prevent warping and cracking.

Because wood is porous, it absorbs a lot of moisture. When it dries out, the wood may be rough because the water has raised the grain. We recommend that you periodically clean and oil cutting boards to restore their smooth surfaces and to protect them from moisture.

Some salad bowls are finished with a waterproof varnish, but many people prefer to keep their bowls untreated to absorb seasonings and enhance the flavor of the salad.

Wipe woodenware immediately after using it with a sponge or paper towel moistened in cold water. If the item needs to be washed, don't let it soak in water and never put it in the dishwasher. Always wash woodenware quickly; then rinse immediately, wipe dry, and air-dry thoroughly before storing.

Remove stains from woodenware with a solution of ¼ cup chlorine bleach and 1 quart warm water. Rinse and dry, then coat with vegetable oil. Get rid of odors by rubbing the surface with a slice of lemon.

WOODENWARE CLEANER

Baking soda cleans and deodorizes wood. Mix ½ cup baking soda with 1 quart warm water and rub it on the wood surface.

Caution: Wear rubber gloves. Use a synthetic scouring pad to clean a cutting board. Scour the gummy residue on the edges of the board. Rinse with clear water, blot the moisture with a towel, and air-dry completely. Bring back the natural wood finish by giving woodenware a coat of boiled linseed oil, salad-bowl finishing oil, or vegetable oil, rubbed in with a synthetic scouring pad. Apply two thin coats 24 hours apart, wiping off the excess a half hour after each application.

CHAPTER 6

Bathrooms

If there's a growing collection of dust balls under your bed or a month's worth of newspapers on your coffee table, you can live with that. But a grimy bathroom is another story. If there is one cleaning job that really must be done each week no matter what, it's cleaning the bathroom. But you can make this task a whole lot easier if you and everyone else who uses the bathroom quick-cleans it every day.

Bathrooms tend to become both dirty and messy. The obvious solution to bathroom clutter is to create storage for the things most bathrooms are not designed to store, such as makeup, hair dryers, electric shavers, and magazines.

Clear countertops not only look better, but they are quicker to clean, because there's no clutter to clean around and under. But even the most well designed bathroom is prone to soap scum and streaky surfaces. The most efficient way to clean your bathroom is to clean it often.

Most bathrooms are made of materials that are easy to keep clean. Tile and porcelain surfaces are stain-resistant if dirt and scum are not allowed to build up on them. Make it a firm rule in your home to rinse out the tub or shower stall immediately after you use it. Rinse it while you are still wet and in the tub or stall. Simply spray water from the shower head on all interior surfaces, then lather soap onto a damp sponge, swish it around the tub or stall, and rinse. The basin can be given a similar treatment each evening by the last person who uses it.

Keeping tile and porcelain surfaces clean so that they never need to be scoured not only saves time, but it also protects these surfaces from unnecessary wear and keeps them looking their best. Most scouring powders and nonabrasive cleaners will safely rid tile and porcelain surfaces of dirt, but if stains have to be removed with harsh abrasives, the porcelain or ceramic tile will be scratched. These tiny scratches invite more dirt build-up, and your cleaning problems increase.

The toilet and floor can wait for a weekly cleaning. Wash the floor after you have completed all the other bathroom-cleaning chores.

BATHTUBS AND BASINS

Most bathtubs and basins are made of porcelain. If the fixtures are older, chances are the material is porcelain on cast iron. These fixtures may not be as acid- and alkaline-resistant as newer porcelain-on-steel tubs and basins. Cultured marble is also used for one-piece basin/countertops. Fiberglass tubs, which are lighter and easier to install than steel tubs, are used in new-home construction and remodeling, but they are not as durable as porcelain-coated steel. If you have a fiberglass tub, you will have to be especially careful when you clean it to avoid scratching the surface.

CLEANER FOR BATHTUBS AND BASINS

This solution cleans porcelain as well as cultured-marble and fiberglass fixtures. Mix 1/2 cup vinegar, 1 cup clear ammonia, and 1/4 cup baking soda in 1 gallon hot water.

Caution: Wear rubber gloves, and work in a well-ventilated area when using this powerful solution. Apply the solution to the fixtures with a sponge, scrubbing if necessary, and rinse with clear water.

Since it is better to keep a bathtub clean than to scour it periodically, we suggest that you add bubble bath or a capful of detergent to your bathwater to prevent bathtub rings. If you prefer a clear-water bath, you can remove rings while the water drains from the tub by rubbing a nylon-net ball or pad around the tub. Keep your ring-eliminator in the soap dish.

Porcelain basins and tubs should be cleaned with powdered cleanser or nonabrasive liquid cleanser. Sprinkle a mild abrasive powder on a damp sponge and apply it to the porcelain surface of the tub or basin. Use a synthetic scouring pad on stubborn soil. Rinse with clear water. When you clean the bathtub and basin, also remove hair from the traps in the drains to prevent clogging.

Cultured-marble or fiberglass tubs and basins should be cleaned with a commercial fiberglass-cleaning product or nonabrasive liquid cleanser. Apply either product with a damp sponge and rinse with clear water.

If you have an older bathroom, rust stains are often a problem. We've found that commercial rust removers are very effective. **Caution:** Wear rubber gloves when you work with these products because they contain acid. You can also clean discolored porcelain fixtures with a paste made of cream of tartar moistened with hydrogen peroxide or a paste made of borax moistened with lemon juice.

Scrub the paste into lightly stained areas with a brush, and rinse well.

If your old porcelain bathtub has yellowed, try rubbing the tub with a solution of salt and turpentine. **Caution:** Wear rubber gloves when you work with this solution. Rinse well.

When you're down on your knees scrubbing the bathtub and get a closeup view of a grimy rubber or vinyl bathtub mat, don't waste time scouring the mat. Just toss it into your clothes washer with several bath towels. The terry cloth scrubs the mat, and everything will come out clean.

COUNTERTOPS

Bathroom countertops are sloshed, splotched, and splattered with everything from hair spray to shoe polish. In most homes, countertops are made of materials that can stand up to the assault: ceramic tile, cultured marble, and plastic laminate. Because these materials are durable, they are easy to clean.

Ceramic Tile

Glazed ceramic tile is virtually stain-proof, but this isn't true of the grout between the tiles, which is porous and soft. To compound the problem, grout is often white to contrast with dark tiles or to match gleaming, white tiles. Either way, stained or mildewed grout is very noticeable and makes your whole bathroom look grubby.

A toothbrush or nailbrush is the best tool for cleaning grout. To remove mildew, dip the brush in chlorine bleach and gently scrub the affected grout. If spots persist, hide them. We've found

you can camouflage stained grout with a white fingernail pencil or white liquid shoe polish. (If you get shoe polish on the tiles, let it dry, and then wipe it off with a

GROUT CLEANER

Put 3 cups baking soda in a medium-size bowl and add 1 cup warm water. Mix to form a smooth paste. Scrub it into the grout with a damp sponge or toothbrush, and rinse thoroughly after cleaning. Mix a fresh batch for each cleaning session.

CERAMIC-TILE CLEANER

Mix $\frac{1}{2}$ cup cup vinegar, 1 cup clear ammonia, $\frac{1}{4}$ cup baking soda, and 1 gallon warm water.

Caution: Wear rubber gloves, and work in a well-ventilated area when using this powerful solution. Apply it to the countertop with a sponge, and rinse with clear water. Wipe dry to prevent water spots. Mix a fresh batch of this cleaner for each cleaning session.

damp rag.) Even though ceramic tile resists dirt and rarely needs cleaning, you may sometimes have to clean it; so here are a few suggestions:

- Never use harsh abrasive cleaners that might scratch the glaze.

- If you use an aerosol-foam or spray tile-and-grout cleaner, follow the manufacturer's instructions, and rinse with clear water to finish the job.

- Sparkle your bathroom walls and countertops by rubbing the ceramic tile with car wax, and buff after 10 minutes.

Cultured Marble

Cultured marble resembles real marble, but it is a lot more versatile and much easier to care for. Unlike plastic laminate, cultured marble is not a thin veneer; if you

scratch or burn it, you can often repair the damage.

We recommend that you avoid using abrasive cleaners and steel-wool pads to clean cultured marble; they will scratch the surface, making it difficult to keep clean. Mildly abrasive liquid and powdered cleansers should be applied directly to the wet surface of the countertop to dissolve dirt and soap film. Rinse well, and buff dry with a soft cloth.

CULTURED-MARBLE CLEANER

Mix ½ cup vinegar, 1 clear ammonia, and ¼ cup baking soda in 1 gallon hot water.

Caution: Wear rubber gloves, and work in a well-ventilated area when using this powerful solution. Apply it to the cultured marble with a sponge, rinse with clear water, and buff dry. Dirt and soap film are quickly and inexpensively removed with this mixture.

Plastic Laminate

Plastic laminate is very durable if you don't scratch it, chip it, knock off its edges, burn it, scrub it, let water seep under it, stain it, or otherwise mistreat it. Plastic laminate is made of thin layers of plastic superimposed on craft paper and overlaid on particle board or plywood.

The color of most plastic laminate is only in the top layer. The glossy, matte, or textured surface is also laid on. This is the reason plastic laminate cannot be restored if it is damaged; all its beauty is on the surface.

We regularly apply an appliance wax or light furniture wax to protect and brighten plastic-laminate surfaces.

During your weekly bathroom-cleaning session, wipe your plastic-laminate countertop with a damp cloth or sponge. We've found that a two-sided scrubbing pad with fiber on one side and a sponge on the other works especially well. Moistened slightly with water, the fiber side is just abrasive enough to loosen greasy smears and other soil. Turning the scrubber over, use the sponge side to wipe the surface damp-dry. When a spot or stain persists, first sprinkle baking soda on the spot and scrub gently.

If this doesn't take care of the problem, apply a polishing cleanser with a wet sponge.

DRAINS

In most homes, the bathroom sink is a dressing table as well as a washbasin, and everyone in the family shampoos in the shower. Hair and soap are washed into bathroom drains day and night, and the cruddy mess can quickly jam up the works. All that is needed to clean some clogged drains is to clear the trap of hair and soap curds. Regular clearing of the traps saves your plumbing, and it also cuts down on cleaning time, since when water flows out of the basin and tub quickly, it doesn't allow dirt to settle on these surfaces.

When clearing the trap doesn't clear the drain, you'll have to take stronger measures. First, use a plumber's helper and plunge the drain. (We suggest that you keep one handy in the bathroom.) Before you use the plunger in the bathroom basin, plug the overflow opening. This allows the plunger to exercise its maximum suction effect on the clogged drain.

If plunging does not open the drain, use a chemical drain opener. These products must be handled with special care because they are caustic and harmful to skin and eyes. Use them in a well-ventilated area, and follow the manufacturer's instructions. Commercial drain openers are sold in granular, liquid, and pressurized forms. Granular products utilize lye to do their work, liquid drain openers use lye and other chemicals, and pressurized products work by chlorofluorocarbon propellants and pressure. If you use a granular drain opener, you must first remove standing water from the sink; this is not necessary for liquid and pressurized products. Chemical drain openers will damage porcelain enamel and should not be allowed to remain on the surface of your fixtures for any length of time.

DRAIN OPENER

Moderately clogged drains sometimes can be opened by pouring 1/2 cup baking soda, followed by 1/2 cup vinegar, down the drain.

Caution: The interaction of these two ingredients creates foaming and fumes, so replace the drain cover loosely. Flush the drain with clear water after about 3 hours.

If the first type of chemical drain opener you use does not work, do not use a different chemical drain cleaner unless the initial cleaner has been flushed away totally. Never use a plunger or a pressurized drain opener after using a chemical cleaner; it may cause dangerous chemicals to splash back onto you. Also, be sure to tell your plumber what you have put into the drain before he or she starts to work. The combination of ammonia and other household cleaners with chemical drain openers produces hazardous gases.

HARDWARE

If you get into the habit of wiping the sink and tub hardware after each use, you'll prevent water spots and keep your bathroom looking sparkling longer. You don't need to do anything special to care for most bathroom hardware—just clean it along with the tub and basin, using the same cleaning products and methods. Rinse well, and buff with a dry cloth.

Clogged shower heads are a common problem if you have hard water. You don't have to replace them, but you'll have to take them apart for cleaning. Remove the head from its fitting, dismantle it, and soak it in vinegar. Use a toothbrush to brush away mineral deposits. Clean the holes by poking them with a wire, pin, toothpick, or ice pick.

We've found that the fastest way to clean chromium and stainless steel is with baking soda applied to the surface with a dry cloth. It will remove fingerprints, smudges, and sticky residue with no further rinsing or wiping.

Treat wooden towel racks with an occasional application of furniture polish to bring up the shine and give a protective coating. Apply the polish with a soft cloth, and buff.

BATHROOM MIRRORS

The better your family's dental hygiene, the sooner you'll see spots before your eyes when you look in the bathroom mirror. As is true

of other bathroom surfaces, daily wiping both delays and facilitates heavy-duty cleaning. You can quickly remove spots and spatters from a mirror with a damp facial tissue, and then polish it with a dry one.

If your mirror is clouded by hair spray, rubbing alcohol will wipe away the haze.

MIRROR CLEANER

Mix ⅓ cup clear ammonia in 1 gallon warm water. Apply with a sponge/squeegee or pour it into a pump bottle and spray sparingly onto the mirror. Buff with a lint-free cloth, chamois, or paper toweling. Vinegar may be substituted for ammonia.

During the morning rush hour, if you're trying to shave while the shower is producing billows of steam in the same small bathroom, you can defog the bathroom mirror quickly by blowing hot air on it with a hair dryer. Running an inch of cold water in the bathtub before adding hot water eliminates fogging altogether.

Refer to **Chapter 4, Inside Your Living Areas** for additional mirror cleaning tips and cleaners.

SHOWER CURTAINS

Shower curtains need to be cleaned on a regular basis to remove built-up soap scum and water deposits. All shower curtains are washable; fabric curtains and some plastic ones can be washed in the machine. Use your regular laundry detergent when you wash fabric shower curtains, and follow the manufacturer's instructions for water temperature and wash/rinse cycles. When you machine wash plastic shower curtains, use the gentle cycle and cool water. Wash plastic curtains in 1/2 cup detergent and 1/2 cup baking soda, along with two large bath towels. To prevent a machine-washed shower curtain from wrinkling, add a cup of vinegar to the rinse cycle.

Washing a plastic shower curtain in the bathtub causes fewer wrinkles than machine washing. We've found a good method for doing this. Mix 1/2 cup vinegar, 1 cup clear ammonia, 1/4 cup baking soda, and 1 gallon hot water, and apply the solution to the shower curtain with a sponge while it is lying flat in the bathtub. **Caution:** Wear rubber gloves, and work in a well-ventilated area when using this powerful solution. Let stand a few minutes to loosen the scum, and then scrub the curtain with a sponge or brush, adding more cleaner if necessary. Rinse well in warm water to which a few drops of mineral oil have been added; this will keep the curtain soft and flexible. Shake off excess water and hang to drip-dry.

Back fabric curtains with a plastic liner to preserve their good looks and to make them more effective. You can also back a new plastic shower curtain with your old plastic shower curtain. Hang the new curtain on the same hooks, but in front of the old curtain.

SHOWER-STALL CLEANER

Mix 1/2 cup vinegar, 1 cup ammonia, 1/4 cup baking soda, and 1 gallon hot water.

Caution: Wear rubber gloves, and work in a well-ventilated area when using this powerful solution. Apply it to the walls of the shower with a sponge, scrubbing with a brush if necessary to remove all the scum. Rinse well with clear water and wipe dry.

The old curtain will take the beating from water and soap scum while the new one stays clean.

Mildew often develops on shower curtains. To discourage its growth, spray clean curtains with disinfectant. Make it your habit to shake excess water off the shower curtain after each use.

SHOWER ENCLOSURES

Shower stalls would be self-cleaning, if soap scum, mildew, and mineral deposits didn't build up on the shower enclosure. We've collected the following helpful hints to make dealing with these cleaning chores easier:

- Clean glass shower doors with a sponge dipped in white vinegar.

- Leave the shower door open slightly to allow air to circulate; this will discourage the growth of mildew.

- If the grout or caulking in your shower breaks away where the walls join the tub or shower floor, recaulk immediately to prevent water damage.

- If your shower area is subject to mildew, spray it periodically with a mildew inhibitor and disinfectant.

- Remove hard-water deposits on shower enclosures with a solution of white vinegar and water.

- Remove water spots on the metal frames around shower doors and enclosures with lemon oil.

TOILETS

Cleaning the toilet is one of those grin-and-bear-it chores that you want to get through as quickly as possible. Many toilet-bowl cleaners and deodorizers claim that they'll help you do this. Some products are truly helpful, some are not. Most cleaners that are placed in the tank and are dispensed each time the toilet is flushed do little more than color the water. Some clean the bowl better than plain water, but in-tank cleaners are not a substitute for a regular scrubbing, when you also clean the seat and the rim of the toilet bowl.

Toilet bowls and tanks usually are made of vitreous china, which is nonporous and easy to clean. Before you clean your toilet, read the label on your cleaning product to learn its exact chemical makeup and how it should be used. Be especially careful never to mix products that contain chlorine bleach with ammonia-based products. Always wear rubber gloves when you work with toilet cleaners. They contain strong

chemicals and should be flushed immediately after the bowl has been cleaned. You should be careful not to allow cleaners to remain in the toilet or to touch other bathroom surfaces. Keep a long-handled brush for cleaning only toilet bowls.

The exterior of a toilet should be cleaned with the same products you use for tubs and basins. Wipe the toilet seat, the tank, around the rim, and around the base when you clean.

TOILET-BOWL CLEANERS

Clean and disinfect your toilet bowl with 1/2 cup chlorine bleach. Pour it into the bowl, and let it stand for 10 minutes. Then scrub with the toilet brush, and flush. **Caution:** Wear rubber gloves, and do not mix chlorine bleach with any other cleaner.

CHAPTER 7

Laundry

When we think about laundry, we often imagine snow-white sheets billowing in the breeze, shirts with no telltale stains or rings around the collars, glimmering little-league uniforms, and baby-soft, sweet-smelling piles of neatly folded clothes. The reality of laundry is less exciting. But if you don't keep up with the laundry, you won't have anything to wear. Since you have to do it, make it as easy as you can. We're here to help speed you through piles of laundry, with guidelines and tips on how to care for everything from your favorite sweatshirt to your best shirt.

UNDERSTANDING FABRIC CARE LABELS

The first step toward doing your laundry quickly and efficiently is to know what an item is made of and the best way to care for it. Most garments and many other fabric items manufactured and sold in the United States have permanently attached care labels. These labels are also required on garments made of suede and leather.

They can be of enormous help in determining exactly how you should remove stains and clean an item.

Certain information is not always included on care labels. Neither the manufacturer nor the retailer is required to inform a consumer that a certain fabric will shrink.

The label assumes that the purchaser knows that an item labeled "hand wash" should be washed in lukewarm water and that *all* nonwhite articles should not be treated with chlorine bleach.

Another important piece of information contained on fabric care labels is the fiber content of the material. This is especially important with blends. These fabrics are combinations of fibers, such as cotton and wool, cotton and polyester, or wool and acrylic. Blends should be cared for in the same way as the fiber with the *highest percentage in the blend.* For example, a blend of 60 percent cotton and 40 percent polyester should be cleaned as though it were 100 percent cotton. However, when you remove spots and stains, you should follow procedures recommended for the *most delicate fiber in the blend.* For example, to remove stains from a blend of cotton and silk, use the procedure recommended for silk. If after such treatment the stain is still apparent, follow the procedure for cotton, the most durable fiber in this blend.

NATURAL FABRICS

Cotton

Cotton fabric is strong, long-wearing, and absorbent. It will shrink and wrinkle unless it is given special treatment. Cotton is often blended with other fibers or treated with a finish to make it wrinkle-resistant. It is available in a wide variety of weights and textures, from denim or corduroy to percale.

Machine wash and tumble-dry cotton fabrics, using a water temperature ranging from cold to hot, depending on the manufacturer's care instructions, and an all-purpose detergent. If needed, a chlorine bleach can be used on white or colorfast cotton unless a fabric finish has been applied.

You should never use more than the recommended amount of bleach; this can damage the fibers.

We recommend that you use fabric softener to improve softness and to reduce wrinkling. But fabric softener makes cotton less absorbent and should not be used on towels, washcloths, or diapers.

Pretreat oil-based spots and stains with a prewash.

Wash and shrink cotton fabrics before using them for home sewing.

Iron cotton with a hot iron for best results and use spray starch or spray sizing to restore its crisp appearance.

Linen

Pure linen fabric wrinkles easily, so many manufacturers make linen blends or add wrinkle-resistant finishes to overcome this problem. Linen is absorbent and comfortable to wear, but it can crack or show wear at the seams, along the creases, and at the finished edges of the garment.

Machine wash and tumble-dry linen. An all-purpose detergent is the best cleaning agent, and chlorine bleach can be used on white linen. Follow the manufacturer's recommended amount so as not to damage the fabric.

Linen can also be dry-cleaned. It should be pressed with a hot iron while it is still slightly damp for the best results.

Silk

Silk is a delight to wear, but it requires special care. Most silk garments are marked "dry-clean only." However, some silk can be washed by hand. A piece of silk fabric that you are going to make into a garment should first be washed by hand.

We suggest that you always test a corner of the fabric for colorfastness before washing a whole piece of silk. Some dyed silk will bleed.

Use a hair shampoo containing protein and warm or cool water for hand washing; the protein in the shampoo feeds the protein in the silk. Handle washable silk gently during washing; never twist or wring it. Hang silk out of direct sunlight to drip-dry.

Press silk while it is still damp with a warm iron (below 275 degrees Fahrenheit) or use a steam iron. To remove stains from washable white or light-colored silk, use only oxygen bleach or mix 1 part hydrogen peroxide (3 percent) to 8 parts water.

Wool

Wool fabric is highly resilient, absorbent, and sheds wrinkles well, but wool will shrink and mat if it's exposed to heat and rubbing. Popular in both knit and woven fabrics, the textures of wool fabrics range from fine wool crepe and jersey to felt and mohair.

We recommend that you treat spots and stains on wool fabrics with solvent-based spot removers. Clean felt by wiping it with a dry sponge. For a more thorough treatment, hold the material over steam from a teakettle, and brush lightly with a dry sponge or lint-free cloth to smooth the surface.

Always dry-clean wool unless it is specifically marked "washable."

Use light-duty detergent in cold water to wash wool. Allow the article to soak for a few minutes before starting the washing process. Handle woolens carefully when they are wet to avoid stretching. Machine washing is appropriate only if the care label indicates that it is, and then use only cold water and the gentle cycle.

Remove excess moisture by rolling a wool article in a towel. Then block it into shape and dry it on a flat surface. Only machine-dry woolens if the manufacturer's instructions recommend it. Press wool with a hot iron, using lots of steam. Cover the article with a damp cloth or chemically treated press cloth. Allow the garment to dry thoroughly before storing it.

SYNTHETIC FABRICS

Acetate

Acetate is made from cellulose and has a silk-like appearance. Closely related to rayon, it has good body and drapes well. Taffeta, satin, crepe, brocade, and double knits often contain acetate. It is not very absorbent or colorfast, and acetate loses its strength when it is wet.

Hand wash acetate carefully in warm water, using a light-duty detergent, if the care label specifies that the article is washable; otherwise have it dry-cleaned. Do not soak colored items or wash them with white articles. We suggest that you add fabric softener to the rinse water to reduce wrinkles.

Line-dry acetate away from heat or direct sunlight. Press at the coolest setting, on the wrong side, while the article is damp. Use a press cloth when pressing the right side of the fabric.

Nail-polish remover and perfumes will permanently damage acetate.

Acrylic

Many acrylic weaves resemble wool's softness, bulk, and fluffiness. Acrylics are wrinkle-resistant and usually are machine washable. Often acrylic fibers are blended with wool or polyester fibers. Acrylic's biggest drawback is its tendency to pill. Blends will do this less than pure acrylic.

Dry-clean acrylic garments or wash them by hand or in the machine. Pretreat oil-based stains, and turn garments inside out before laundering to reduce pilling.

Take care to wash delicate acrylic items by hand in warm water, gently squeezing out the water. Machine wash sturdy acrylic articles with an all-purpose detergent, and tumble-dry at low temperatures.

If the fabric is labeled "colorfast," it can be bleached with either chlorine or oxygen bleach. We've found that adding fabric softener to the rinse water every third or fourth time an article is washed reduces static electricity.

Press at a moderate temperature setting, using steam.

Nylon

Nylon fabrics are extremely strong, lightweight, smooth, and lustrous. They are also nonabsorbent and have excellent resistance to abrasion and wrinkles. Often combined with spandex, nylon knits are very stretchy but hold and recover their original shape. Available in many textures, nylon is used to make all kinds of items, including lingerie, carpets, rainwear, and tents.

Always follow the manufacturer's cleaning instructions. Pretreat oil-based stains on nylon. Machine wash sturdy articles in warm water with an all-purpose detergent. Hand wash lingerie and hosiery, using warm water and light-duty detergent, or machine wash in a mesh bag to prevent stretching or tearing. Do not launder white nylon with colored fabrics of any kind.

Use a chlorine bleach only if a nylon article is colorfast, and use fabric softener to reduce static electricity. Tumble-dry nylon at a low temperature setting. Press at a cool temperature setting.

Polyester

Polyester fabrics are strong, resilient, wrinkle-resistant, colorfast, and crisp. They hold pleats and creases well, but they are also nonabsorbent, attract and hold oil-based stains, may pill when rubbed, and may yellow with age. Polyester is used for clothing and filling; some bed linens and towels are also made from polyester blends.

Polyester can be safely dry-cleaned or machine washed. Pretreat oil-based stains with prewash or all-purpose liquid detergent. We recommend that you turn polyester-knit garments inside out before washing to prevent snags. Machine wash polyester in warm water using an all-purpose detergent, and tumble-dry at a low temperature setting. Use a chlorine bleach if necessary. Using a fabric softener will reduce static electricity.

Do not overdry polyester; this will cause gradual shrinkage. Press polyester fabrics at a moderate temperature setting or use steam.

Rayon

Rayon is a strong, absorbent fabric, but it tends to lose its strength when it is wet. It is used for drapery and upholstery fabrics as well as for clothing.

Dry-clean rayon or wash it by hand unless it is labeled "machine washable." For hand wash, use lukewarm water with a light-duty detergent. Machine wash rayon in warm water on a gentle cycle with a light-duty detergent. Squeeze moisture out gently when washing rayon fabrics by hand. Chlorine bleach can be used on rayon unless it has been treated with a resin finish.

Drip-dry and press rayon on the wrong side with an iron at a medium temperature setting while the fabric is damp.

Spandex

Spandex is a lightweight fiber that resembles rubber in durability. It has good stretch and recovery, and it is resistant to damage from sunlight, abrasion, and oils. Always blended with other fibers, spandex provides the stretch in waistbands, foundation garments, swimwear, and dancewear.

Pretreat oil-based stains. Hand or machine wash spandex-blend garments in warm water using an all-purpose detergent. Do not wash white spandex with colored fabrics of any kind. Use only oxygen or sodium-perborate bleach. Rinse thoroughly.

Garments made with spandex can be line-dried or tumble-dried on low. Press clothing that contains spandex rapidly, if needed, using a low temperature setting.

Triacetate

Triacetate resembles acetate, but it is less sensitive to heat. This allows triacetate to be creased and crisply pleated. Triacetate is often a component in jersey, textured knits, and taffeta.

Pleated garments can be hand or machine washed in cold water. Set the gentle cycle to agitate for 3 minutes. Drip-dry permanently pleated garments, or air-dry them in dryer.

Most triacetate articles can be machine washed with an all-purpose detergent in hot or warm water. Tumble- or line-dry triacetate. Press, if necessary, using a hot temperature setting.

LAUNDRY TECHNIQUES

You could jam all your dirty laundry in the washing machine, run it through whatever wash cycle happens to be programmed, and hope for the best. This method may leave your sweater doll-sized or turn your white silk shirt pink, but it's quick—if you don't count the time you'll spend replacing your ruined clothes. Doing your laundry properly will take more time. Your clothes will last longer and look better if you pay careful attention to sorting, pretreating, water temperature, machine cycle, and the right laundry products for each particular fabric.

Sorting

Properly sorting the laundry is the first step to a clean wash and helps to keep your clothes, linens, and other household items looking their best through repeated washings.

Color

First sort the laundry by color. Put all the white or predominantly white articles in one pile, the light colors and pastels in another pile, and the bright and dark-colored items into a third. Then separate the dark pile into two piles: one for colorfast items and one for noncolorfast items.

Degree of Soil

Separate each pile into three smaller piles: lightly soiled, moderately soiled, and heavily soiled.

Compatible Loads

Now you have up to 12 various-sized piles of laundry. Combine or divide the piles to come up with compatible, washer-sized loads.

The following hints will help you with your final sorting:

- Combine white and light-colored items that have similar degrees of soil into the same pile.

- Combine noncolorfast items with similarly colored colorfast items with the same degree of soil.

- Separate synthetics, blends, and permanent-press fabrics from natural-fiber fabrics without special finishes.

- Create a separate pile for delicate items that must be hand washed.

- Separate white synthetic articles, and wash them only with other white fabrics.

- Separate items made from fabrics that produce lint, such as chenille robes and bath towels, from fabrics that attract lint, such as corduroy, knits, synthetics, and permanent press.

Preparing the Wash

Follow these hints to minimize damage to the articles you are washing and to help clean them thoroughly:

- Save care information so you can follow the recommended cleaning procedures.

- Know the fiber content and finishes of fabrics so you can select the proper water temperature and cleaning products.

- Close all zippers, hook all hooks, and button all buttons.

- Turn pockets inside out to get rid of debris.

- Remove nonwashable trim or decorations and pins or buckles that might make holes or snag other articles in the wash.

- Tie or buckle all belts and sashes to prevent tangling.

- Pretreat spots, stains, and heavily soiled items with pre wash spot-and-stain remover, liquid detergent, a paste made from granular soap or detergent, a bar of soap, or a presoak solution.

- Mend seams, tears, holes, or loose hems to prevent further damage during the wash cycle.

- Turn sweaters and corduroy garments inside out to prevent pilling and to combat their tendency to collect lint.

Prewash Spot-and-Stain Removers
While soaps and detergents can be worked directly into spots and heavily soiled areas before you put the laundry into the washer, a special product designed just for removing spots and stains is more convenient to use. Called prewash spot-and-stain removers, these aerosols or pump sprays are excellent for spot treating stubborn soil, especially grease marks on synthetic fabrics.

Treat the stain while it is still fresh. Saturate the soiled area completely, then lightly rub the fabric together to work the prewash product into the fibers.

Some prewash products can damage the exterior finish of your washer and dryer, so be careful where you spray them.

Presoaks

Granular presoak products containing enzymes break down some stubborn stains such as milk, blood, baby formula, chocolate, gravy, fruits and vegetables, and grass. Presoaks are not effective on rust, ink, oil, or grease.

Following the manufacturer's directions, mix a solution in a large sink or in the washer. Before adding the soiled laundry, make sure that the presoak has dissolved thoroughly. Soak clothes for the recommended length of time; an overnight soak is suitable for articles that look dull and dingy. Do not soak dark- and light-colored fabrics together for long periods of time; this can cause colors to run. Wash the laundry as usual after using a presoak.

Laundry Products

Most commercial laundry preparations are designed to be used in washing machines, but some can be used for both hand and machine washing. Read the label carefully before purchasing any product to make sure it is the right one for the job you want it to do. When you use a laundry product, follow the directions precisely and measure accurately.

Water Conditioners

The amount and type of chemicals and minerals dissolved in water determines whether it is hard or soft. The condition of the water affects the cleaning potential of laundry products: The softer the water, the more effective it is for cleaning. Determine the hardness of your water so you will know if you need to condition it for effective cleaning.

Hard water leaves a residue on articles you launder; this is known as *washing film*. To soften water, the minerals must be removed or chemically locked up. Water that measures under four grains hardness per gallon will probably clean effectively, especially if a detergent rather than soap is used. You can soften hard water with a mechanical water softener that attaches to your home's water tank or by adding a water-conditioning product to the wash and rinse water. Follow the directions on product labels precisely.

Wash flame-retardant items only in soft water.

Use a water conditioner to remove previously formed washing film or soap/detergent buildup. You can also remove hard-water washing film from diapers, towels, or fabrics by soaking them in a solution of 1 cup white vinegar and 1 gallon water in a plastic container.

Detergents and Soaps

Soap is a mixture of alkalis and fats that is a good cleaner in soft water, breaks down well in city sewer systems, and does not harm the environment. Soap is less effective in hard water, however, because it reacts with the high mineral content to form soap curd, which leaves a gray scum on clothing.

Detergents are synthetic washing products derived from petroleum and other nonfatty materials. They are less affected by hard water than soap and have excellent cleaning power. Since detergents contain a wetting agent that lifts off dirt and agents that help to make hard water minerals inactive, they do not create scum.

Always follow the manufacturer's instructions for the amount of detergent to use, the proper wash cycle, and the recommended water temperature. Measure carefully, but use extra detergent for heavy and/or greasy soil, larger-than-normal loads, and warm- or cold-water washes. You may also need more than the manufacturer's recommended amount of detergent if you have hard water and when you use phosphate-free detergent. Adding 1 cup ammonia to the wash water will boost detergent effectiveness for heavily soiled or greasy wash loads.

Use liquid detergents in cold-water washes for best results, or dissolve powder or granular detergents in 1 quart hot water, then add the solution to the cold wash water.

Bleach

Bleach works with detergent or soap to remove stains and soil, whiten white items, and brighten the colors of some fabrics. It also acts as a mild disinfectant.

The two basic types of laundry bleach are chlorine and oxygen. Common liquid chlorine bleach is the most effective and least expensive, but it cannot be used on all fabrics. Oxygen bleach is safer for all washable fabrics, resin-finished fibers, and most washable colors, but it is much less strong than chlorine bleach.

Always give colored fabrics a colorfastness test before using any bleach by mixing 1 tablespoon chlorine bleach with ¼ cup warm water or 1 tablespoon oxygen bleach with 2 quarts hot water. Apply the solution to an inconspicuous place; wait a few minutes and check for a color change. If the color does not bleed, use the bleach according to the manufacturer's directions.

Add diluted chlorine bleach to the wash water about five minutes after the wash cycle has begun or use the automatic bleach dispenser if your washer is equipped with one. Bleach clothes only in the wash cycle so the bleach can be completely removed during the rinse cycle. Hot water improves the performance of bleach.

Fabric Softeners

Fabric softeners add softness and fluffiness, reduce static electricity on synthetics so they will not cling, help decrease lint, and make pressing easier. They are available in liquid, sheet, or solid form. Liquid fabric softener is added to the wash or rinse cycle; sheet and solid products are used in the dryer.

Read the instructions for using a fabric softener to determine at what time in the laundering cycle to add it. Dilute liquid fabric softeners with water before adding them to the automatic fabric-softener dispenser or to the rinse.

Fabric softener can stain fabric if it is poured or sprayed directly onto clothes or if it is used with a water conditioner. Sheet fabric softeners will stain polyester articles if they are used in the dryer when these fabrics are drying. If you stain an item with fabric softener, rub the stained area with liquid detergent or a prewash spot-and-stain remover and rewash the article.

USING AN AUTOMATIC CLOTHES WASHER

For the best results from your washing machine, you must know how to combine multiple load capacities, water levels, temperature settings, and cycles properly.

Loading the Machine

Read the washer manufacturer's instruction booklet thoroughly, put it away in a safe place for reference, and follow the recommended laundry procedures.

Do not overload the machine; garments should not pile up past the top of the agitator. Mix small and large items in each load for the best circulation, and distribute the load evenly around the wash basket. Loading the

washer to full capacity each time you wash will save time and energy. But don't be tempted to throw your dark bath towels in a bleach load or your sweaters in a permanent-press load just to fill it.

Water Temperature

The correct water temperature(s) for a load of wash varies according to the kinds of fabric being washed and the amount of soil. Use the following chart to help you select the proper wash and rinse temperature settings. Be aware of the actual temperature of the water in your washing machine; it can vary during the year. If the water temperature is below 80 degrees Fahrenheit, it is too cold to do a good job even if you use a cold-water detergent. Adjust the amounts of cold and hot water flowing into your

Continued on page 172.

Type of Load	Wash Temperature	Rinse Temperature
White and light-colored cottons and linens Diapers Heavily soiled permanent-press and wash-and-wear fabrics All other greasy or heavily soiled wash	130° F.-150° F. (hot)	warm or cold
Dark colors Lightly and moderately soiled permanent-press and wash-and-wear fabrics Some woven or knit synthetic fabrics (see care label) Some washable woolens (see care label) Any other moderately soiled wash	100° F.-110° F. (warm)	cold
Noncolorfast fabrics Some washable woolens (see care label) Some woven or knit synthetic fabrics (see care label) Fragile items Bright colors Any lightly soiled wash	80° F.-100° F. (cold)	cold

machine to get the water within the correct temperature range for each temperature setting.

Water Level

Use enough water to provide good circulation, but do not use so much that you waste water and energy. Most machines have a water-level control, and you should adjust this control to match each load you wash. Refer to the manufacturer's instructions for this information.

Machine Cycles

Select the type of cycle according to the kind of load and the degree of soil (see chart below). Follow these guidelines, using a longer cycle for heavily soiled laundry.

HAND WASHING

We recommend that you never disregard the "hand wash only" label even when you're in a hurry.

Sort hand wash in the same way you sort machine wash. Separate

Type of Load	Cycle
Sturdy white and colorfast items	Normal
Sturdy noncolorfast items	Normal
Sturdy permanent-press and wash-and-wear fabrics	Permanent-press
Delicate fabrics and knits	Gentle or delicate

the clothes into piles by color, putting white and light colors together, dark and noncolorfast items into separate piles. Pretreat stains and heavily soiled areas with prewash spot-and-stain remover or by rubbing liquid detergent into the area.

Use light-duty soap or detergent and dissolve it in warm or cool wash water before adding the clothes. Submerge the articles in the water and let them soak for 3 to 5 minutes. Gently squeeze the suds through the fabric, being careful not to rub, twist, or wring excessively. Rinse articles thoroughly in cool water until the water runs clear. Add a few drops of fabric softener to the last rinse if desired.

Hang blouses, dresses, scarves, and lingerie to drip-dry. The shower is a good place for this. Use towels to blot excess moisture from sweaters, stockings, panties, and bras. Hang these items to dry only if the weight of the water will not stretch them out of shape; otherwise, dry them on a towel on a flat surface.

DRYING CLOTHES

Most clothes dried in an automatic dryer come out soft and almost wrinkle-free. If you have time and a backyard, you may prefer to dry your laundry on the clothesline on sunny days, reserving the dryer for inclement weather and for your permanent-press fabrics.

Machine Drying

Read the manufacturer's instruction booklet to familiarize yourself with your dryer's operating procedures and recommended cycles.

Shake out each article before placing it in the dryer to speed the drying time and cut down on wrinkles. Do not overload the dryer; this will cause uneven drying and excessive wrinkling. Remove items from the dryer as soon as it stops, and hang or fold them to keep them from getting wrinkled. Dry clothes until they are "almost dry" rather than "bone dry" if you are going to iron them. Clean the lint filter after each use of the dryer.

Line-Drying

If you are going to the trouble to hang your clothes outside to dry, make sure that your clothespins and clotheslines are clean and free of rust. You can wash plastic clothespins in mild soap and warm water in an automatic clothes washer, using a mesh bag. Wash wooden clothespins in a hot dishwashing-detergent solution. Use plastic rope or plastic-coated wire for

your clothesline, and wipe it with a damp cloth before using it.

Attach items to the clothesline by their most sturdy edges. Smooth the clothes as you hang them, running your fingers down seams and along the front, collar, and cuff edges. Dry white and light-colored items in the sun and bright-colored items in the shade.

SOLVING LAUNDRY PROBLEMS

Here are some of the most common laundry problems and simple, quick ways to solve them.

Brown Stains

Cause: Soap, detergent, or bleach reacting with iron or manganese in the water.

Solution: Install an iron filter on your water system. Do not use chlorine bleach in the wash. Use a water conditioner in both the wash and rinse water.

Excessive Wear

Cause: Improper use of bleach.

Solution: Always dilute chlorine bleach before adding it to the washer.

Cause: Tears, holes, snags, split seams, and loose hems.

Solution: Make all repairs before washing an item and hook all hooks, close zippers, and remove pins or other sharp objects before putting articles in the washer.

Gray and Dingy Fabric

Cause: Insufficient detergent, incorrect sorting, or water temperature too low.

Solution: Follow our suggestions for sorting and proper washing techniques.

Greasy Spots

Cause: Undiluted liquid fabric softener coming into contact with fabric.

Solution: Dilute liquid fabric softeners before adding them to the rinse or softener dispenser.

Cause: Hard water.

Solution: Use a water conditioner appropriate for your detergent or install a mechanical water softener.

Cause: Fabric softener sheets in the dryer with lightweight fabrics.

Solution: Use liquid softener in the washing machine when cleaning delicate fabrics. Greasy spots can be removed by rubbing in liquid detergent and then washing again.

Also use a lower temperature setting on the dryer.

Cause: Overloaded washer.

Solution: Reduce the load size so the clothes can circulate in the water more freely.

Harsh-Feeling Fabrics

Cause: Spin speed not adequate.

Solution: Increase the spin speed or check to make sure the load is balanced so the spin can reach its maximum speed.

Cause: Hard water.

Solution: Increase the amount of detergent, install a mechanical water softener, or use a water-conditioning product.

Cause: Using soap in hard water.

Solution: Switch to a detergent,

install a mechanical water softener, or use a water conditioner.

Linting

Cause: Incorrect sorting.

Solution: Read and follow our suggestions for sorting.

Cause: Not enough detergent.

Solution: Increase the amount of detergent to help hold lint in suspension so it can be flushed down the drain.

Cause: Overloaded washer.

Solution: Reduce load size or increase the water level so the wash can circulate freely.

Cause: Improper use of fabric softener.

Solution: Do not add softener directly to wash water unless specifically directed to do so.

Cause: Debris in cuffs or pockets.

Solution: Remove any tissues, paper, or loose dirt before washing.

Scorching During Ironing

Cause: Iron temperature setting too high.

Solution: Check recommended heat on garment tag and reduce the temperature setting on the iron accordingly.

Cause: Heat of iron reacting with a buildup of laundry products.

Solution: Run clothes through one or two complete washing cycles with 1 cup water conditioner and no other laundry product, then wash as usual.

Static Electricity

Cause: Synthetic fabrics tend to produce static electricity.

Solution: Use a fabric softener in your washer or dryer.

Yellowing

Cause: Incomplete removal of soil, especially body oils.

Solution: Pretreat heavily soiled areas, increase the amount of detergent, use hotter water, and use bleach.

Cause: Iron in the water.

Solution: Install an iron filter, use extra detergent, and use water conditioner.

Cause: Aging of some fabrics.

Solution: No solution except the above suggestions for routine washing to slow the aging process.

CHAPTER 8

Cars

Cleaning and maintaining the original appearance of your car may not be high on your list of favorite ways to spend your weekend, but we've found that it is time well spent. You can expect to obtain more at trade-in time or when you sell your car if you've helped your car to keep its good looks. Your car is a very large investment, and keeping it looking as new as possible protects that investment. In this chapter, we'll show you how to clean your car—inside and out.

CARPETS

Keeping the carpet in your car clean is almost impossible: There's no place to wipe your feet before you get in. Mats offer some protection from dirt and grime, and we suggest that you install them in a new car as soon as you buy it and replace them when they become worn. But even when you use mats to protect the carpeting, dirt and grime inevitably accumulate in the carpet fibers.

Vacuum the carpeting in your car frequently to remove the grit and soil that can break down carpet fibers and cause unnecessary wear. A handheld cordless vacuum is especially good for vacuuming your car, and its recharging stand can be mounted right in your garage so it's conveniently at hand. We recommend that every time you vacuum the car, you remove the mats, shake them thoroughly, and vacuum them as well.

Spills in the car are not like spills in the house. When you turn a corner too fast and spill your morning coffee, you can't stop in the middle of traffic and clean up the mess. But you should try to wipe up spills soon after they occur. We suggest that you keep paper towels and a whisk broom in the car and accessible for emergency cleanups.

Make it your habit to roll up your car windows whenever you park your car outside. If rain or water from the neighbor's lawn sprinkler leaks into your car and soaks the carpet, it is difficult to dry it out, and mildew can set in quickly.

When the carpeting in your car needs to be cleaned, use a spray or spray-foam carpet cleaner. Some manufacturers make carpet-cleaning products especially for cars. Read and follow the instructions for the best results. Vacuum the carpet after cleaning only when it is completely dry.

CARPET CLEANER

Salt residues can be removed from carpets with a solution made of equal parts vinegar and water. Apply the mixture with a sponge, but do not overwet the carpeting. Allow the carpet to dry thoroughly, then vacuum.

CHROME

Shiny chrome adds sparkle to a car's appearance, and chrome must be cleaned and polished regularly to prevent rust and corrosion. Polish chrome after the car has been washed. Remove rust spots with a steel-wool pad or a piece of crumpled aluminum foil. Wax chrome trim when you wax the car's body. Use a different cloth to polish the chrome than you use for the body.

Residues of salt will pit chrome. Have your car washed frequently during the winter when the roads have been salted, and hose off salt residues when the temperature is above freezing.

Many commercial chrome cleaners and polishes are available. If you use one, follow the manufacturer's instructions for the best results.

CHROME CLEANER

Dip a moistened sponge into baking soda and rub onto the chrome. Let it sit for a minute, then rinse, and buff the chrome dry with a soft cloth. Use a synthetic scouring pad with the soda for particularly stubborn spots.

FLOOR MATS

Rubber mats give your automobile's carpet essential protection from excessive wear. We recommend that you clean the mats every time you wash your car. Even though it may take a bit of extra effort, you should clean car mats frequently in the winter, because they accumulate salt and sand when it's snowy. Use a stiff-bristled brush and scrub them with a detergent solution. Do not use harsh chemicals, solvents, or steel wool to clean the mats; these cleaners will damage the rubber. After washing the mats, apply a rubber protectant or liquid-wax shoe polish.

FLOOR-MAT CLEANER

Mix 3 tablespoons mild dishwashing detergent in 1 gallon warm water. Gently scrub the mats until all the dirt and grime has been removed. Allow the mats to dry thoroughly on both sides before replacing them in your car.

PAINT

Drive-through car washes are convenient and many use the proper techniques to clean and protect a car's finish. But some use strong detergents that can eventually ruin the finish. Washing your car yourself is a safe alternative to high-priced car washes. You can achieve professional results by washing, drying, and waxing your car by hand with the right equipment and methods.

Move your car to a shaded spot; washing or waxing a car in the hot sun or when the surface is hot may cause streaking and may damage the finish. Close all the car windows tightly before starting to wash your car. Then thoroughly hose off the dust and loose dirt; brushing it off with a cloth or even with your hand may scratch the finish. Use a garden nozzle on the hose that provides strong water pressure. Spray the wheels, hubcaps, undersurface of the fenders (avoid wetting the engine compartment), bumpers, and as far under the chassis as possible, using a hard stream of water to remove dirt, mud, and salt.

We recommend that you use mild dishwashing liquid or commercial car shampoo to clean your car. Remember that you are using cold water and will need to use plenty of detergent. Apply the cleaning solution with a clean, soft sponge, mitt, or cloth, scrubbing lightly where necessary. Work from the top down. Wash one area at a time, but keep water running over the entire car so that the dirt slides off rather than being scrubbed in.

Use a cleaner, automotive rubbing compound, or cleaner/wax on older cars to help remove the oxidized layer. Remove tar deposits with special tar remover. You can also remove tar, as well as bird droppings and insects, with a cloth saturated with vegetable oil. Hold the cloth on the dirty area until the material lifts off with gentle rubbing.

Rinse the car before the suds dry. You may have to work quickly to do this on hot days and in dry climates.

Dry the car with a soft, absorbent terry-cloth towel or a chamois to prevent water spots. Paper towels can scratch automobile finishes. They should not be used to dry the exterior of the car except the windows. When water no longer beads up on the car's surface, apply wax or polish, following the manufacturer's instructions. After the wax has dried, sprinkle baking soda or cornstarch on the surface. Either powder will pick up the wax and help bring out surface luster. If dried wax remains around the chrome trim, remove it with a soft-bristled brush.

TIRES

Wash tires and hubcaps after the rest of the car has been washed. Hose them with a hard stream of water to remove loose dirt before scrubbing.

Use a special tire brush or a sponge to remove soil and pebbles from the tires and the spokes of the hubcaps. Tires can be cleaned with all-purpose cleaners, steel-wool soap pads, and special whitewall cleaners. A synthetic scouring pad should be used to remove black scuff marks from whitewalls. Alloy hubcaps must be treated especially gently because their surfaces are easily damaged.

Coat the cleaned tires with a rubber protectant to help maintain a shiny appearance and to minimize rubber deterioration. Self-polishing floor wax will also make tires shine.

UPHOLSTERY

Cloth

Care should be taken to avoid spots and spills on cloth upholstery because it is not easy to clean. Mop up all spills as soon as possible, and spot treat them to avoid stains. Always carry paper towels in your car to absorb spills.

Vacuum cloth upholstery, using a cordless vacuum or the upholstery brush attachment. We recommend that you use a crevice tool to pick up dirt from hard-to-reach places.

Any commercial upholstery shampoo can be used to clean automobile upholstery. Follow the manufacturer's instructions, and vacuum thoroughly when the product is completely dry.

Vinyl and Leather

Vinyl upholstery is durable and

easy to care for. Leather upholstery is a luxury-car option, but the care for both kinds of upholstery is the same.

Vacuum the creases and crevices of your car's upholstery as part of your routine, general car care, but be especially careful not to scratch the upholstery with sharp-edged attachments or by exerting too much pressure. Use a whisk broom to remove loose soil or debris when

you are unable to vacuum. Clean upholstery with a commercial product or a homemade solution. Use a leather or vinyl conditioner periodically to prevent cracking, drying out, and fading. When you use a commercial product, read and follow the manufacturer's instructions.

LEATHER OR VINYL UPHOLSTERY CLEANER

Make a warm, soapy solution using soap flakes and water. Apply the suds to the upholstery with a soft-bristled brush, working the cleaner gently into the grain. Wipe the upholstery clean with a damp sponge, and buff it dry with a soft cloth.

CLEANER FOR VINYL CAR TOPS

Pour ⅛ cup dishwashing detergent into a pail, and add a hard stream of about 1 gallon warm water to make lots of suds. Apply the solution with a sponge and scrub with a brush. Rinse well, wipe dry, and apply a vinyl dressing for protection.

WINDOWS AND WINDSHIELDS

Clean all exterior glass and plastic windows each time you refuel your car. Use a synthetic scouring pad to remove stubborn street grime and bugs. Make sure that the cloth with which you wipe the windows is free of grit that can scratch the surface. Ideally, you should use only a full-skin chamois; it will not streak and is unlikely to scratch your car windows.

Each time you wash the car, clean the glass and plastic windows inside and out with a glass-cleaning product or windshield-washer fluid. Clean the inside of the windows with strokes in one direction and the outside with strokes in another direction; this makes it easy to find and correct streaks.

To properly care for your windshield, always use specially formulated windshield-washer fluid. Keep the washer jets clear and adjusted so that they spray onto the windshield correctly. Replace windshield-wiper blades when they begin to smear or skip on the windshield. We've found that the blades will last longer if you always wet the windshield before using the wipers.

CAR-WINDOW CLEANER

Mix ¼ cup vinegar in 1 gallon warm water. Wipe the windows inside and out with a cloth dipped in the solution. Then wipe with a clean, dry cloth. This solution also cleans plastic car windows.

CHAPTER 9
Beat Spots and Stains

Unusual and not-so-unusual spots and stains find their way onto your carpeting, your clothes, your furniture, and the other surfaces in your home. Each stain requires its own special treatment, or you may end up with a worse mess than you started with.

In this chapter, we want to share with you some basic information about stains and stain-removal. We'll give you a comprehensive shopping list of cleaning tools and products that you will want to have in your stain-removal kit to combat stains, and we'll teach you the eight basic techniques of stain-removal.

THREE KINDS OF STAINS
Greasy Stains

You can sometimes remove grease spots from washable fabrics by laundering. Pretreating by rubbing detergent directly into the spot often helps, as does using dry-cleaning solution on the stain. If you are treating an old stain or one that has been ironed, a yellow stain may remain after treatment with a solvent. Bleach can sometimes remove this yellow residue.

To remove grease spots from nonwashable fabrics, sponge the stain with dry-cleaning solution. Elimination of the stain may require several applications. Allow the spot to dry completely between spongings. Greasy stains may also be removed from nonwashable fabrics by using an absorbent, such as cornstarch, cornmeal, French chalk, or fuller's earth. Dust the absorbent on the greasy spot. When it begins to look caked, it should be shaken or brushed off.

Absorbents are easy to use and will not harm fabrics. However, other stain-removal agents, such as detergents, dry-cleaning solvents, and bleach, can damage fibers. Before using any of these products, you should carefully read the care label on the stained item and the label on the product container. If you do not have either one of these labels, we recommend that you test the cleaning product on the fabric in an inconspicuous area.

Nongreasy Stains

Fruit juice on your collar, black coffee on your lapel, tea on your pocket flap, food coloring on your cuff, ink on your pant leg—nongreasy stains are easy to acquire, but not impossible to remove. If you are treating a nongreasy stain on a washable fabric, we recommend that you sponge the stain with cool water as soon as possible. If this doesn't remove the stain, try soaking the fabric in cool water. The stain may soak out within half an hour, or you may need to leave the item in water overnight. If some of the stain still remains after this treatment, try gently rubbing liquid detergent into it, then rinse with cool water. The very last resort is to use bleach, but always read the fabric-care label before you bleach. If the stain is old or has already been ironed, it may be impossible to remove it completely.

A nongreasy stain on fabric that cannot be washed can be sponged with cool water. Place an absorbent pad under the stained area and slowly drip water through the fabric with a pump/trigger spray bottle or an eye dropper. This method of flushing the stain lets you control the amount of water and the rate at which it flows through the fabric so that you don't inadvertently spread the stain. If you treat a nongreasy stain with water while it is still fresh, you often can remove it entirely. If water alone fails to remove the stain, work liquid detergent into the stain and rinse it by sponging or flushing with cool water. Sponge the spot with

rubbing alcohol after you've rinsed it to remove detergent residue and to speed drying. (**Caution:** If you're treating acetate, acrylic, modacrylic, rayon, triacetate, or vinyl, be sure to dilute the alcohol with water, 1 part alcohol to 2 parts water.)

Combination Stains

Some stains are double trouble. Coffee with cream, salad dressing, and lipstick leave a combination of stains behind them; they're both greasy and nongreasy. Getting rid of combination stains is a two-part operation. First get rid of the nongreasy stain and then attack the greasy residue. On most fabrics, you'll need to sponge the stain with cool water, then work liquid detergent into the stain and rinse thoroughly. After the fabric has dried, apply dry-cleaning solution to the greasy part of the stain. Allow the fabric to dry.

TAKING THE STRESS OUT OF STAINS

There's a surefire strategy for beating stains. You'll save time by doing it right the first time rather than wasting time experimenting with various cures for the problem and possibly making the stain worse than it was to start with.

Here are the basic rules:

- The quicker the better. The best time to treat a stain is the moment after it occurs. The longer it sets, the more likely it is that a stain will become a permanent one.

- Be gentle. Rubbing, folding, wringing, and squeezing cause stains to penetrate more deeply and may damage delicate fibers.

- Know what you're cleaning. Identify both the staining agent and the stained surface. Both will affect the way in which you treat the stain.

- Clean it off before you clean it. Remove as much of the staining agent as you possibly can before you begin the stain-removal process.

- Keep it cool. Avoid using hot water, high-heat clothes dryers, and irons on stains; heat makes some stains impossible to remove.

- Always follow directions. Read manufacturers' care labels and directions on product containers before you start to clean a stain.

189

- Pretest stain removers. Even water can damage some fabrics, so test every cleaner you plan to use in an inconspicuous place before you use it on the stain.

- Work from the edges into the center. You won't spread the stain or leave a ring.

YOUR BASIC STAIN-REMOVAL KIT

Being prepared is the best way to beat stains. Your well-stocked stain-removal kit, like a first-aid kit, should be ready to help you handle cleaning emergencies whenever they occur.

Here are the tools you'll need to have in your kit:

- Clean, white cotton cloths

- A small brush

- White blotting paper

- White paper towels

- Disposable diapers for absorbing flushed cleaning solutions

- A spoon, blunt knife, or spatula for scraping

- An eyedropper or trigger spray bottle

- Several colorfast weights

Your kit will also need to include a variety of stain-removal agents. What you need depends on what you are likely to have to clean. You will be able to purchase most of them at your local hardware store, grocery store, or pharmacy.

Absorbents

Absorbents "soak up" grease stains. We consider cornmeal the best absorbent for light colors, and fuller's earth the best for dark colors. Spread the absorbent on the stained areas and allow it to work. As the grease is soaked up, the absorbent material will cake or become gummy. It should then be shaken or brushed off. You should repeat the process until the stain has been removed. This may take as long as eight hours or more.

Bleaches

Chlorine

Commonly used to bleach white cotton, linen, and synthetic fabrics, chlorine bleach is a powerful stain remover, which can weaken fibers if it is allowed to stay on fabric for too long a time.

Never use chlorine bleach on silk, wool, or fabrics that are exposed to sunlight, such as curtains. Test chlorine bleach in an inconspicuous place before bleaching an entire item. **Caution:** Chlorine bleach is poisonous. If it comes in contact with skin or eyes, it will cause burns and irritation.

Color Remover

Hydrosulfite, the active chemical compound in color removers, lightens the color of fabric before it is redyed a lighter color. This chemical also removes some stains from colorfast fibers. Always pretest color remover. If the product causes a distinct color change instead of fading the fabric, you may be able to restore the original color by rinsing immediately with cool water. If the color fades when color remover is applied, the original color cannot be restored.

Color remover should never be used in a metal container. **Caution:** Color removers are poisonous. Avoid prolonged contact with skin. Observe all precautions on the label.

Hydrogen Peroxide

The 3-percent solution of hydrogen peroxide that is sold as a mild antiseptic is a safe bleach for most fibers. A stronger solution used for lightening hair is too strong to use on fabric and other household surfaces. Buy peroxide in small quantities and store it in a cool, dark place; it loses strength quickly after it is opened and if it is exposed to light.

Sodium Perborate

You may purchase sodium perborate in crystal form at pharmacies under trade names or generically. It is safe for all fabrics and surfaces. This oxygen bleach is slower-acting than hydrogen peroxide. When you use this bleach, be sure that you rinse the treated articles thoroughly in clear water.

Chemicals

Acetic Acid

You can buy acetic acid in a 10-percent solution at pharmacies. White vinegar is a 5-percent acetic acid and can be used as a substitute for the stronger solution.

Acetic acid is a clear fluid, used full strength to remove stains on silk and wool. It must be diluted with 2 parts water for use on cotton and linen. (We recommend that you test for colorfastness.) Never use this chemical on acetate. If acetic acid causes a color change, try sponging the affected areas with ammonia; this may restore the color.

Acetone

Fingernail-polish remover and household-cement thinner are acetone based, but they should not be substituted for pure acetone because they contain other ingredients that may worsen the stain. You can purchase acetone at pharmacies and paint stores. The colorless liquid can be used on stains caused by substances such as fingernail polish or household cement. Although acetone will damage neither natural fibers nor most synthetics, it should be tested to make sure that dyed fabrics will not be harmed. Acetone should not be used on fabrics containing acetate; it will dissolve them.

Caution: Acetone is flammable and evaporates rapidly, producing toxic fumes. When using acetone, work outside or in a well-ventilated area. Avoid inhaling the fumes. Store acetone in a tightly capped container in a cool place.

Alcohol

Isopropyl alcohol in a 70-percent solution is sufficient for most stain-removal jobs that call for alcohol. Stronger, denatured alcohol (90-percent solution) can also be used. Be sure you do not buy alcohol with added color or fragrance. Since alcohol will fade some dyes, we recommend that you test it on the fabric you will be cleaning. Alcohol will damage acetate, triacetate, modacrylic, and acrylic fibers. If you must use it on fibers in the acetate family, dilute the alcohol with 2 parts water.

Caution: Alcohol is poisonous and flammable.

Ammonia

Use plain household ammonia without added color or fragrance for stain removal. Because ammonia affects some dyes, we recommend that you test it on the stained article. To restore color changed by ammonia, rinse the affected area in water and apply a few drops of white vinegar, then rinse with clear water. Ammonia damages silk and wool; if you must use it on these fibers, dilute it with an equal amount of water and use as sparingly as possible. **Caution:** Ammonia is poisonous. Avoid inhaling its fumes. It will cause burns or irritation if it comes in contact with skin or eyes.

Coconut Oil

You can buy coconut oil in drug and health-food stores. It is used in the preparation of dry spotter that is used to remove many kinds of stains. If you cannot obtain coconut oil, you may substitute mineral oil, which is almost as effective.

To make dry spotter, combine 1 part coconut oil and 8 parts liquid dry-cleaning solvent. Store this solution in a tightly capped container to prevent evaporation.

Glycerine

Use glycerine in the preparation of wet spotter that is used to remove many kinds of stains. To make wet spotter, mix 1 part glycerine, 1 part white dishwashing detergent, and 8 parts water. Store the solution in a plastic squeeze bottle, and shake well before each use.

Oxalic Acid

Effective in treating ink and rust stains, oxalic acid crystals are sold in many pharmacies. The crystals must be dissolved in water (1 tablespoon crystals to 1 cup warm water). Test the solution on a hidden corner of the spotted item before using it on the stain. Moisten the stained area with the solution. Allow it to dry, then reapply. Be sure all traces of the solution are rinsed out. **Caution:** Oxalic acid is poisonous. Wear rubber gloves and avoid contact with skin and eyes.

Sodium Thiosulfate

Also known as photographic "hypo" or "fixer," sodium thiosulfate is available in crystal form at drugstores and photo-supply houses.

Although considered safe for all fibers and harmless to dyes, this chemical should be tested on an inconspicuous area before use.

Turpentine

Most often used as a thinner for oil-based paints, turpentine is effective on paint and grease stains. **Caution:** Turpentine is flammable and poisonous. Observe all the precautions stated on the label.

Vinegar

When you use vinegar on a stain, you should always use white (clear) vinegar. Cider and red-wine vinegar have color that can leave a stain. Vinegar is a 5-percent acetic acid solution and should be diluted if you use it on cotton or linen. Vinegar is safe for all other colorfast fibers, but it can change the color of some dyes, so always test it on an inconspicuous area first. If an article changes color, rinse the affected area with water to which you've added a few drops of ammonia. Rinse thoroughly with clear water. This may restore the color.

Washing Agents

Detergents

When our stain-removal directions call for a mild detergent, choose a white dishwashing liquid; the dyes in nonwhite detergents may worsen the stain.

When instructions call for a pretreating paste made of detergent and water, use a powdered detergent that does not contain bleach. When the stain-removal directions specify that you should apply a liquid laundry detergent directly to the spot or stain, be sure to read the directions on the product's label carefully. Some products cannot safely be used in this manner. Other detergent products, such as those used in automatic dishwashers or for heavy-duty household cleaning, and certain laundry products may contain alkalies. They can set stains caused by ammonia, soap, and oven cleaner and should not be used for spot removal.

Enzyme Presoaks

Most effective on protein stains, such as those caused by meat juices, eggs, and blood, enzyme presoaks may harm silk and wool. Make sure you have exhausted every alternative before you use enzyme presoaks on these two fabrics. Use a presoak as soon as possible after mixing with water; enzyme-presoak solutions become inactive in storage. Be sure to read and observe all the directions on the product label.

Powdered Cleansers

Scouring powders and baking soda can be used to remove stains on surfaces that will not be harmed by abrasives. However, you should be aware that prolonged or overly vigorous scrubbing with these products can scratch even the most durable surface. Make sure you rinse away all the powder when the job is completed.

Pretreaters

Use pretreaters on spots and stains when you think that a stain might not respond to normal laundering procedures. Pretreaters start the cleaning process before the stained item is put in the washer.

They must be used in conjunction with the rest of the laundering process; do not try to use a pretreater alone, as though it were a spot remover. After applying a pretreater, you should not allow the fabric to dry out before you begin washing.

Soaps

Bath soaps with added moisturizers, fragrance, dyes, or deodorant should not be used to treat spots. Purchase either laundry soap or pure white soap.

SAFETY PRECAUTIONS

Many of the products you stock in your stain-removal kit are flammable or toxic, and certain safety tips should be kept in mind when storing and using these products.

- Follow the directions on the product label and heed all warnings.

- Store stain-removing products carefully and out of the reach of children. The storage area should be cool, dry, and separate from food storage areas. Keep bottles tightly capped and boxes closed.

- Do not transfer cleaning products to new containers so that they are always clearly labeled and you never have to search for directions for their proper use.

- Glass and unchipped porcelain containers are preferable to metal or plastic when working with stain-removal agents. Never use plastic with solvents. Never use any container that is rusty. Clean all containers thoroughly after use.

- Protect your hands with rubber gloves. Don't touch your eyes or skin while handling stain-removal chemicals. If you do accidentally touch your eyes or spill chemicals on your skin, flush immediately with clear water.

- Remember that the fumes of solvents are toxic; work in a well-ventilated area.

- Do not use chemicals near an open flame or electrical outlet. Never smoke while using chemicals.

- Do not use a solvent as a laundry additive.

- When using a solvent on a washable fabric, be sure to rinse all traces of the solvent out of the fabric.

- Never combine products unless specifically directed to do so in the recipes for homemade cleaning solutions in this book.

Many combinations can be dangerous.

- If the cleaning process requires the use of more than one stain-removal agent, rinse out each product thoroughly before applying the next.

EIGHT WAYS TO BEAT STAINS

We would all like to be able to squirt a little dab of the right solution on a stain, stand back, and watch the spot fade away forever. Unfortunately, stain removal has not yet become quite that simple. But can beat the stain with a combination of the right techniques and the right cleaning solutions. We have already discussed the cleaning supplies you need to have on hand in your stain-removal kit, but you also need to know how these tools and products are used to remove stains quickly and effectively.

There are eight basic techniques for stain removal: brushing, flushing, freezing, presoaking, pretreating, scraping, sponging, and tamping. The right technique for a particular spot or stain depends on what was spilled and where it fell.

Brushing

Use brushing to remove dried stains. Some kinds of spots, such as dried mud, can be removed completely by brushing. For other kinds of stains, brushing is only a step in the cleaning process.

We recommend a small, stiff-bristled brush for this technique. When you're working on fabric, stretch the piece on a firm, clean surface. Hold a sheet of paper next to the stain, and brush the staining material onto the paper. A gentle motion with the brush pulls the stain up off the surface and onto the paper.

Flushing

Use flushing to remove loosened staining materials and the residue from stain-removal agents. If cleaning products are left in the material, they may cause additional staining or even damage the treated article.

When you are flushing a stain, especially one on nonwashable fabric, you need to control the flow of water carefully so that you don't spread the stain or get the fabric wetter than you need to. An eyedropper or a trigger spray bottle that can be adjusted to a fine stream lets you precisely control the amount of liquid flushed through the fabric. Before you begin this treatment, place a clean absorbent pad, such as a disposable diaper, under the spot. Then slowly and carefully apply water or the recommended stain remover to the stain. Work slowly so that you don't flood the pad with more liquid than it can absorb. Replace the absorbent pad frequently to prevent restaining the fabric.

If you're treating a stain on a washable fabric, rinse the article in warm water after you have flushed the stain.

Freezing

Candle wax, chewing gum, and other gooey substances are easier to remove when they are cold and hard. Hold an ice cube against the stain to freeze it. If the stained item is not washable, place the ice in a plastic bag. You can put a small stained item in a plastic bag and place the whole thing in the freezer. After the stain has solidified, it can usually be gently lifted or scraped from the surface.

Presoaking

When your wash is grayed, yellowed, or heavily soiled, washing alone will not get it clean and bright—you will have to presoak. Sort the soiled items before presoaking; items that are not colorfast should be presoaked separately from colorfast items because their colors may bleed.

You may add bleach, laundry detergent, or an enzyme presoak to the soaking water. But don't use chlorine bleach and an enzyme product at the same time. You can leave colorfast, stained articles in a presoak for as long as it takes to get them clean, but for most stains, 30 minutes is long enough. Items that aren't colorfast should be soaked only briefly.

Remember, before you wash a load of presoaked laundry, make sure that it has been thoroughly rinsed and that no residue of the presoak is left on the items.

Pretreating

Pretreat oily, greasy stains with liquid laundry detergent, a stain removing spray, bar soap, or a pretreating paste made from powdered detergent and water. After you apply a pretreater, rub it into the stain gently, and wash the item as you would normally.

Scraping

Scrape away solid staining material with a dull knife, spoon, or spatula before you apply stain remover. Don't press too hard; move the edge of your scraping tool back and forth across the stain in short strokes.

Sponging

Put an absorbent pad, such as a disposable diaper, under the stain before you sponge it. On a carpet you will have to work without an absorbent pad, so be especially careful not to use excessive amounts of cleaning solution or water. Use another pad or a sponge to apply the stain-removing agent.

Sponge the stain gently using light strokes. Change either pad as soon as any of the stain is deposited on it.

Some fabrics, such as acetate, triacetate, and rayon, are likely to develop rings when they are sponged. When you work on stains on these fabrics, barely wet the pad with stain remover and touch the fabric lightly so that the stain remover is absorbed as slowly as possible. Blot the treated area between absorbent pads. Allow it to air-dry. Ironing or drying with heat may cause the stain remover itself to stain the fabric.

Tamping

The best way to get some stains out of durable, tightly woven fabrics is to tamp them with a soft-bristled brush.

CHAPTER 10
Hints for Your Home

Most of us want to get through our cleaning as quickly as possible, so we can get back to doing all the other things we need and want to do. But there are some things that have to be done around our homes that we like to slow down and enjoy doing. We want to do these little extras because they'll improve the quality of our lives. In this chapter, you'll find a collection of helpful hints from people who have figured out better ways to do things around their homes. When you read some of these terrific tips, you'll probably say to yourself that that's the way you've always done it. When you read others, you may find yourself asking why you never thought of that.

GENERAL PAINTING TIPS

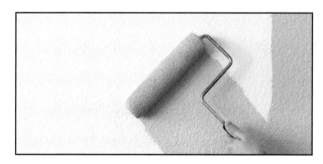

Record how much paint is required to cover each room by writing the amount on the back of the light-switch plate. When you remove the switch plate before repainting, you'll be reminded of how much paint you need.

When painting a ceiling with a roller, it's not necessary to try to keep the roller strokes all the same length. The lines won't show when the paint dries.

If you use masking tape around windows while painting the woodwork, remove the masking tape immediately after painting. Otherwise, it may pull off some of the paint.

If you want to paint a window frame and have no masking tape, use strips of dampened newspaper. They will stick to the glass. Peel off the paper when you finish each frame.

To get paint drips off hard-surface flooring, wrap a cloth around a putty knife and gently scrape up the paint.

Then wash the areas with warm, soapy water. Don't use solvent; it can damage the finish on the floor.

If you're interrupted in the middle of a painting job, wrap aluminum foil or plastic wrap around your brushes and rollers. The wrapping should be loose enough to avoid mashing the bristles on brushes or the pile on rollers but tight enough to keep the air out. Leave the wrapped brushes on a flat surface or hang them up. Put the packet in the freezer to save the brush for a longer period of time.

Prevent drips when painting a drawer front by removing the drawer and painting it face up.

If you can't—or don't want to—remove hardware when painting adjacent areas, coat the hardware with petroleum jelly before painting. You'll be able to wipe off any paint that accidentally gets on the metal.

To avoid smearing while painting cabinets, paint the insides of the cabinets first. Then paint the tops, bottoms, and sides of doors before painting the door fronts. If you proceed in this sequence, you won't have to reach over already-painted areas.

Protect doorknobs when painting a door by wrapping the knobs with aluminum foil or by slipping plastic sandwich bags over them.

When painting stairs, paint alternate steps so that you'll have a way out. When those steps dry, paint the others. Or paint one side of each step at a time. Use the other side for foot traffic until the painted side dries, then reverse the process.

To avoid painting a window shut, gently slide the sash up and down as the paint hardens but before it forms a seal.

If your light-switch plate was painted over along with the wall and you need to remove it, avoid flaking or chipping any paint by cutting carefully around the switch plate with a single-edge razor blade. Remove the screws and lift off the plate.

Don't wipe your paintbrush against the lip of the paint can. The lip will soon fill up with paint that will run down the side and drip off. Use a coffee can to hold the paint instead.

Wrinkling occurs when too much paint is applied or when the paint is too thick. You can correct wrinkling easily by sanding the surface and brushing on paint of a thinner consistency.

Glue paper plates to the bottoms of paint cans to serve as drip catchers. The plates move along with the cans and are more convenient than newspapers.

If the smell of fresh paint bothers you, you can eliminate it from a room in one day with a dish of ammonia, vinegar, or onion slices in water left out in the room.

If you are working on a ladder in front of a closed door, lock the door so that no one can inadvertently swing the door open and send you sprawling.

If you want to be able to use a previous coat of exterior paint as a base for a new coat, the old paint should be no more than five years old. If you wait longer than that you'll be sure to have a major job of scraping, sanding, and spackling.

Artificial light darkens color, so paint will look lighter in the daylight. If you're in doubt about a color at the paint store, take the container outside to examine the color.

Color can saturate your eyes. When mixing paint, look away at a white surface for several minutes to allow your eyes to adjust so that you can judge the color accurately.

To get the correct feel for spray painting and to determine the correct spray distance from the object to be painted, first experiment with a sheet of cardboard as the target area.

Make a paint holder from a coat hanger to keep your hands free when painting. Open the hanger and bend it in half; then bend it into an "S" to hook over the ladder and hold your paint can.

To cut the smell when you're decorating with oil-based paint, stir a spoonful of vanilla extract into each can of paint.

Before using a new paintbrush to apply oil-based paint, soak it for a day in a can of linseed oil. The brush will last longer and be easier to clean.

When tiny spots need a paint touch-up, use a cotton swab instead of a brush. You won't waste paint, and you won't have to clean a brush.

PAINT CLEANUP AND STORAGE

You can remove paint spatters from your hair by rubbing the spots with baby oil.

If you store a partially used can of paint upside down, skin won't form on the surface of the paint. (Be sure the lid is tight.)

Why buy new paint thinner when you can reuse the old? Here's how: Pour paint thinner into an empty coffee can. After you've cleaned your brushes, cover the can tightly and let it stand for several days. When paint from the brushes has settled to the bottom as sediment, drain off the clean thinner into another can and store for reuse.

White paint won't yellow if you stir in a drop of black paint.

Before capping leftover paint for storage, mark the label at the level of the remaining paint so you'll know without opening the can how much is left inside. Label the can with the room the paint was used for, so there's no question which paint to reorder or use for touch-ups.

An empty coffee can with a plastic lid makes a perfect container for soaking brushes. Just make two slits in the center of the plastic lid to form an "X," push the brush handle up through the "X," and replace the lid. The lid seals the can so the solvent can't evaporate, and the brush is suspended without the bristles resting on the bottom.

If you are cleaning brushes or rollers that have been used in oil-based paint, varnish, shellac, or lacquer, work in a well-ventilated area away from open flames.

To clean a paintbrush without making a mess of your hands, pour solvent into a strong, clear plastic bag, and insert the brush. Your hands will stay clean as you work the solvent into the bristles through the plastic.

To avoid having to clean a paint tray, press a sheet of aluminum foil into it before use. When you're finished painting, simply wrap up the foil and dispose of it. You can also line the tray with a plastic bag, and then discard it when the job's done.

Before cleaning a brush, rid it of excess paint by tapping it against the inside rim of the can and then vigorously stroking the brush back and forth on a thick pad of folded newspapers until very little paint comes off.

Rinse all brushes well after washing and shake vigorously to remove excess water. Comb the bristles with a wire brush to straighten them. Then allow the brush to dry completely before storing it flat or hanging from a rack.

To clean a paint roller after use, roll it as dry as possible, first on the newly painted surface and then on several sheets of newspaper. Then slide the roller from its support and clean it with water or a solvent, depending on the type of paint used.

The best brush that money can buy may not last beyond the first job if it is neglected. A brush will give years of service if it is treated properly.

Leftover paint that is lumpy or contains shreds of paint skin can be strained through window screening.

Clean brushes and rollers used for latex paints in water and then wash in a detergent solution. Do not allow brushes to soak in water; this can loosen the bristles.

To keep a brush as soft as new, clean it and then rinse it in a solution of fabric softener and water.

Clean brushes and rollers used for shellac in denatured alcohol, then wash in a detergent solution.

Clean brushes or rollers used for lacquer in lacquer thinner or acetone and then wash in a detergent solution.

Clean brushes or rollers used for oil-based paints and varnishes in turpentine or paint thinner and then wash in a detergent solution.

PICTURES AND MIRRORS

Take the guesswork out of arranging several pictures on a wall. Spread a large sheet of wrapping paper or several taped-together sheets of newspaper on the floor and experiment with frame positions. When you decide on a pleasing grouping, outline the frames on the paper, tape the paper to the wall, and drive hooks through the paper into the wall. Then remove the paper and hang the pictures.

Don't lose a perfect picture grouping when you repaint a room—insert toothpicks in the hook holes and paint right over them; when the paint dries, remove the toothpicks and rehang your pictures.

To prevent a plaster wall from crumbling when driving in a nail or hook, first form an "X" over the nail spot with two strips of masking tape or transparent tape.

Squares of double-faced tape affixed to the two lower-back corners of the frame will keep a picture from moving. If you don't have double-faced tape, make two loops with masking tape, sticky side out. Apply to each of the lower-back corners and press the picture against the wall.

Hang mirrors to reflect you but not the sun; some mirror backings are adversely affected by direct sunlight.

Picture hanging can be frustrating if you simply try to eyeball the right spot to put the hook. Instead, place a picture exactly where you want it the first time with the following method: Cut a sheet of paper to the exact size of the frame. Position the pattern on the back of the picture, pull up taut the wire the picture will hang from, and mark the inverted "V" point on the pattern. Adjust the pattern on the wall, and then poke through it to mark the "V" point on the wall. If you nail the hook there, the picture will hang precisely where you wanted it.

When hanging a mirror with screws that go through mounting holes in the glass, don't tighten the screws all the way. Leave enough play to prevent the mirror from cracking if the wall shifts.

If a picture won't hang straight, wrap masking tape around the wire on both sides of the hook so that the wire can't slip. Or install parallel nails or hooks a short distance apart; two hooks are better than one for keeping pictures in their places.

If the picture isn't too heavy, another timesaving method is to hold the picture itself by its wire and decide where you want it positioned. Wet a fingertip and press it on the wall to mark the wire's inverted "V" point. The fingerprint mark will stay wet long enough for you to drive a nail or hook on target.

If you're hanging a picture from a molding but don't like the look of exposed picture wire, substitute nylon fishing line. The transparent nylon does a disappearing act that allows your picture to star on its own.

Sometimes a picture that has been hanging for a while will leave a dark outline on the wall because dust and dirt have collected against the frame. To prevent this buildup, allow better air circulation by holding pictures slightly away from the wall with thumbtacks pressed firmly into the backs of their frames. You can get the same result by fixing small

tabs of self-sticking foam weather stripping to the picture backing.

Hang heavy objects by driving nails directly into the wood studs behind walls. There are several ways to locate studs. You can tap a wall gently with your knuckles or a hammer. A wall sounds hollow between studs, solid on top of them. Or move an electric razor (turned on) along a wall; a razor registers a different tone over studs. If nails were used to attach drywall to studs, a magnet will indicate the location of the nails and, therefore, the studs.

FLOORS AND FLOOR COVERINGS

Try filling dents in a wood floor with clear nail polish or shellac. Because the floor's color will show through, the dents will not be apparent.

To prevent scratching the floor when moving heavy furniture across uncarpeted areas, slip scraps of carpeting, pile down, under the furniture legs.

If you have a squeaky wood floor under tile or carpet, you may be able to eliminate the squeak without removing the floor covering. Try to reset loose boards by pounding a hammer on a block of scrap wood in the area over the squeaky boards. The pressure may force loose nails back into place.

You may be able to silence a squeaky wood floor by using talcum powder as a dry lubricant. Sprinkle powder over the offending areas, and sweep it back and forth until it filters down between the cracks.

You can remove a floor tile by covering it with dry ice. Wear work gloves to protect your hands. Let the dry ice stand for ten minutes. The cold will make the tile brittle, so it will shatter easily. Chisel out the tile from the edges to the center.

After laying floor tiles, you can help them lie flat by going over them with a rolling pin.

Sometimes you can flatten bulges or curled seams in a linoleum floor by placing aluminum foil over them and ironing them with your iron. (The heat will soften and reactivate the adhesive.) Position weights, such as stacks of books, over treated areas to keep them flat until the adhesive cools and hardens.

To replace a floor tile, lay a piece of aluminum foil on the old tile and then press down with your iron set at medium. The heat of the iron will soften the tile's adhesive, and you can easily pry up the tile with a putty knife or scraper.

Laying floor tile will be easier if the room temperature is at least 70 degrees Fahrenheit before you start, because tile is more pliable at higher temperatures. Put all boxes of tile in the room for at least 24 hours prior to positioning tiles on the floor. Try to keep the room temperature at the same level for about a week after laying the tiles, and then wait at least a week before washing the floor.

If you want to replace a damaged area of sheet flooring, here's a way to make a perfect patch from scrap flooring: Place the scrap piece over the damaged area so that it overlaps sufficiently, and tape it in place. Then cut through both layers at the same time to make a patch that exactly fits the hole. Replace the damaged area with the tightly fitting patch.

DESIGN AND DECORATION

A screen of hanging plants can be a great substitute for curtains.

A room will appear larger if you paint an oversized piece of furniture the same color as the walls.

A small room can be made to look larger if you install mirrors on one wall to reflect the rest of the room.

Small rooms will seem even smaller if filled with elaborate patterns or designs. Keep the furniture for a small room simple and the colors fairly restrained.

The texture of your furnishings can brighten or darken a room. Glossy surfaces like satin, glass, and tile reflect light and add brightness to a room; surfaces like brick, carpet, and burlap absorb light and make a room seem less bright.

In a room with a low ceiling, use vertical lines—high-backed chairs, straight draperies—to carry the eye upward and give an illusion of height.

Horizontal lines—a long sofa or low bookcases—give a feeling of space and make high ceilings appear lower.

A darker color on the ceiling will make a room with a high ceiling seem more in proportion. So will low-placed, eye-catching objects such as a low coffee table, low-slung chairs, and plants on the floor.

To give a room a soft glow, spotlight objects in a room instead of lighting the whole room. For example, light a piece of art or a bookcase.

A favorite painting can be the inspiration for the color scheme of a room. Select one dominant color and several contrasting shades to create a pleasing combination.

There is no need to invest in drapes if your budget is tight. Instead, brighten up inexpensive shades by decorating them with tape to complement the wall color or wallpaper, or by gluing fabric over them.

If you use the same fabric on two different chairs, it will tie the decor of the room together.

If you don't want to buy furniture, you can rent it at surprisingly reasonable rates. Furniture for rent includes everything from sofas and carpets to lamps and works of art.

Matchstick blinds can disguise a wall of hobby or utility shelves for a clean, unified look. They also can be used to partition off a closet or dressing area.

You can make a curtain panel from a bed sheet by knotting the top corners around a bamboo pole.

You'll never have trouble tightening screws and bolts if you remember that, for most, right is tight and left is loose.

An easy way to give a room a new look is to update hardware, such as doorknobs, drawer pulls, and curtain rods.

To add color to matchstick blinds, weave rows of colored ribbon through them.

Turn your bathroom into a miniature gallery with pictures that can't be damaged by humidity.

Look for levelers, mechanical devices built into the furniture's base that compensate for uneven floors, when you buy tall pieces of furniture such as china cabinets and wall units.

Hang shiny, metallic blinds vertically or horizontally to help reflect summer sun. This works especially well in south and west windows.

Keep your decorative baskets looking healthy by placing them away from dry heat and rinsing them periodically with clear water to remove dust and restore moisture.

Furniture upholstered in sturdy fabrics with a high content of durable fibers, such as nylon and olefin, is a good choice for a household with adventurous kids, playful pets, or adults who forget to take off their shoes before putting their feet up on the sofa.

In a long, narrow room, paint the end walls contrasting colors for a striking effect. Room dividers or furniture positioned in the middle of the room will give the effect of two rooms in one and lessen the feeling of length.

To inexpensively add color and interest to your room, display flowers in unusual vases—a crystal ice bucket, a fluted champagne glass, a bright coffee mug, or a jug. Flowers, in fact, look good in almost any container.

For an insulating window covering, attach wood rings to a patchwork quilt and hang it from a wood rod. Don't do this, however, if the quilt is an antique that could fade or otherwise be damaged by exposure to sunlight.

For a quick, easy, and inexpensive way to re-cover a chair, drape a twin-size sheet over the chair, and tie or pin the corners to fit. You can use the same trick to add interest to a small table.

Upholstered furniture should not be placed in constant, direct sunlight or near heating outlets; this can cause fading or discoloration.

Replace the drab cord or chain on a light fixture with a piece of satin piping or silver cord. Thread a bright ceramic bead at the end of the cord for a finishing touch.

A handy deodorizer for wastebaskets: Place a sheet of fabric softener in the bottom of each.

Glue pieces of felt to the rough bottoms of vases and art objects to keep them from scratching tables.

You can make cheap floor rugs by stenciling canvas with nontoxic acrylic paints.

Use leftover dining room wallpaper to make matching place mats. Paste the paper onto sturdy cardboard, trim the edges neatly, and coat each mat with a plastic spray.

Place an unwrapped bar of soap in a drawer or linen closet to give lingerie and linens a pleasant scent.

Make an extra closet into a book nook for quiet reading. Remove the door, and install a wall lamp, shelves, and a comfortable chair.

An old dining table found at a flea market can become a sofa-height coffee table. Just cut the legs to the height you need.

If someone in your family has allergies, check the materials used to fill upholstered furniture before you buy. Most states require furniture manufacturers to attach a label stating the materials used to pad the frame and fill the cushions, such as down, feathers, kapok, horsehair, or polyurethane. If you know one of the materials used is likely to be a problem for an allergy-prone family member, you can avoid that piece of furniture.

You can make unusual centerpieces in no time by floating flowers in clear glass dishes. Fill the dishes halfway with water, cut the stems from the flowers, and place them in the dishes.

Old, carved doorknobs, attached to each end of a dowel, make an attractive curtain rod. Paint or stain the knobs to match your furniture.

STORAGE AND SAVING SPACE

If your home is built with studs and drywall, you can add cabinets between the studs, anywhere you need them—they won't take up any space at all. For example, put a liquor cabinet over your bar, or fashion a canned-goods pantry in your kitchen.

Pegboard is most often used on walls, but it can also be used as a room divider or to make the inside of a closet or cabinet door more functional. When installing pegboard, remember to provide space behind the panels for the hooks.

For extra closet storage, see if your closets can accommodate a second shelf above the existing one. If you install the main clothes-hanging rod high enough, you may be able to install another rod beneath it on which to hang shorter items such as slacks and shirts.

Hang a wicker basket on the bathroom wall for storing towels, tissues, soap, or bath toys.

Use a stairway as a storage area by replacing ordinary nailed-in-place steps with hinged steps. The space under the hinged steps can hold boots or sports equipment.

Glass baby-food jars are ideal for storing nails and screws. Better yet, nail the caps to a wood base or wall plaque, and just screw the jars into place. And remember that partly used tubes of glue and artist's paints won't dry out if they're kept in tightly closed jars.

Hooks, shelves, or hanging bins can transform the insides of closet doors into useful storage areas.

So that you won't misplace frequently used items, glue small magnets on the walls of the medicine cabinet to hold nail files, cuticle scissors, clippers, and other small metal objects.

Add more storage space in your bedroom by building a headboard storage unit. You can place books, lamps, or a radio on the lid of the unit and inside you can store extra linens and blankets.

If your cedar chest or closet no longer smells of cedar, lightly sand its surfaces. Sanding opens the wood's pores and releases a fresh cedar scent. Remember that the scent doesn't kill moths; it merely repels them. So it's best to clean clothes before storing to remove any moth eggs.

Store bed linens, sewing supplies, and infrequently used items in flat, roll-out bins under beds.

Convert an ordinary closet or chest into a cedar closet or chest by installing thin cedar slats over inside surfaces. Then weather-strip to contain the scent.

When storing luggage, put an unwrapped cake of soap inside each one to prevent musty odors from developing.

A hallway can double as a storage area. Line it with shelves or shallow cabinets, or put shelving across the width of the hallway.

Install two rows of coat hooks on your closet doors— one down low for a child to use, another higher up for you to use.

Use the extra slot in your toothbrush holder to keep a medicine spoon handy.

Keep toothbrushes handy but neatly out of the way on cup hooks attached to a wall or under a cabinet.

If you're in need of an extra closet for storing items like golf clubs, skis, and camping equipment, angle a decorative folding screen across a little-used corner.

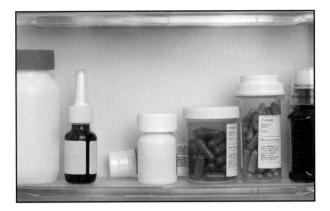

Your medicine cabinet will stay neat and clean with shelf paper made of blotters that can absorb medicine or cosmetic spills.

Hang a basket near the front door and keep your keys in it. You'll always know where they are. Also use this basket for bills and letters that need to be mailed. When you grab your keys, you'll remember to pick up the mail as well.

To increase the capacity and efficiency of a drawer, outfit it with a lift-out tray. Fill the tray with items you frequently use, and use the space beneath the tray for articles you seldom need.

HINTS FOR YOUR HOME

Put the space under a stairway to work as a storage area. Construct a wheeled, wedge-shaped container that fits into the area beneath the steps.

Extension cords won't get tangled when stored in a drawer if you wind them and secure them with rubber bands—or slip them into toilet-paper or paper-towel tubes.

A metal garbage can is perfect for storing long-handled yard tools. Hooks can also be attached to the outside of the can for hanging up smaller tools. You can lift up the whole can and move it to whichever part of the yard you're working in.

Keep your wet umbrella in the shower where it can drip without making a mess. This is an especially useful strategy when you have company on a rainy day and everyone has an umbrella.

To make shelves without hammering a nail, use sturdy boxes stacked on their sides to make compartmented shelf space—you can see at a glance what's stored in the boxes, and you can use the tops for little-used items.

A good place to store small clothing items is in large, metal potato-chip cans—after the cans are washed.

Keep flashlight batteries fresh by storing them in a sealed plastic bag in the refrigerator.

Put a wine rack next to the door and use it to store your sandy beach shoes and muddy running or gardening shoes.

Keep place mats flat and out of the way by hanging them on a clipboard hung from a hook inside a cabinet or pantry door.

If you have trouble with bubbles and creases when applying adhesive-backed paper to shelves or drawers, try smoothing the paper with a blackboard eraser.

To give yourself more storage space in a small bathroom, put up shelves on the dead wall space beside the vanity, over the toilet, or behind the door. Such shelves offer convenient storage without intruding on floor space.

To minimize breakages, store loose light bulbs in tumblers. A paper towel wrapped around the bulb before you put it in the tumbler provides added protection.

YOUR HOME SHOP

A piece of garden hose, slit open, is a handy protective cover for the teeth of a handsaw between projects.

An empty soft-drink carton makes a convenient kit for holding and carrying lubricants.

To protect tools, store them where they aren't subjected to moisture. Keep a thin coating of oil on metal parts, wrap them in plastic wrap, or keep carpenter's chalk, which absorbs moisture, in the toolbox.

To sharpen scissors, snip pieces of sandpaper.

To keep the pores of your hands dirt- or grease-free, wipe on a thin coat of petroleum jelly before starting a messy task.

If you want to remind yourself to unplug an electric drill when changing accessories, fasten the chuck key near the plug end of the cord.

Clean tools without expensive cleaners: Pour a small amount of kerosene onto the metal parts of a tool and rub vigorously with a soap-filled steel-wool pad. Then wad a piece of aluminum foil into a ball and rub on the surface. Wipe away the residue with newspaper, and coat the tool lightly with olive oil before storing. **Caution:** Kerosene is flammable; do not use it near an open flame.

As an aid in measuring lumber or pipe, paint lines a foot apart on your shop or garage floor.

If you hang tools on pegboard walls, outline the tools with paint so you'll know at a glance where each tool goes. You'll also know when a tool hasn't been replaced.

Here's a homemade rust-preventive coating for tools, outdoor furniture, and other metal objects: Combine ¼ cup lanolin and 1 cup petroleum jelly in a double boiler over low heat. Stir until the mixture melts and blends completely, then remove from heat and pour into a clean jar, letting the mixture cool partially. Use the mixture while it's still warm. Don't wipe it off—just let it dry on the object. If you have leftover coating, cover it tightly, and rewarm it before you use it again.

Paint all tool handles with an unusual bright color, or wrap reflective tape around them; they'll be easy to identify if borrowed or left in the wrong place.

Know the exact width of your hand so you can make rough measurements without using a ruler or tape measure.

If you don't have a carpenter's level, you can substitute a straight-sided jar with a lid. Fill the jar three-quarters full of water. Lay it on its side on the surface you're testing—when the water is level, the surface is, too.

You won't waste time when picking up spilled nails, screws, or tacks if you collect them with a magnet covered with a paper towel. When the spilled items snap toward the magnet, gather the towel corners over the pieces and then pull the towel bag away from the magnet.

You can prevent a knot in nylon rope from working loose by holding it briefly over a small flame. The heat will melt and bond the fibers.

Don't take a chance of hitting a thumb or finger when hammering a small brad, tack, or nail. Slip the fastener between the teeth of a pocket comb; the comb holds the nail while you hold the comb. A bobby pin or a paper clip can be used the same way as a comb.

You can often loosen rusted bolts by pouring a carbonated beverage on them.

To prevent metal tubing from denting when sawing it, insert a dowel that fits the tube's interior tightly.

Dipping the ends of a rope in shellac, varnish, or paint will keep them from unraveling.

An old nylon stocking makes an effective strainer if you're out of cheesecloth.

Loosen a stubborn screw, bolt, or nut with a shot of penetrating oil. If you don't have oil, use hydrogen peroxide, white vinegar, kerosene, or household ammonia. If these prove ineffective, heat the metal with an iron, rap it sharply with a hammer while it's still hot, and try again to loosen it.

Caution: Kerosene is flammable; do not use it near an open flame.

If a bolt repeatedly loosens due to vibrations, coat the threads with fingernail polish and reinsert it. When you need to remove it, you can break the seal with a little effort.

For easy workshop measuring, fasten a yardstick to the edge of your workbench. Cut keyhole slots in the yardstick so you can remove it when you need it elsewhere.

You can use a coping saw blade to remove a broken-off key from a lock. Slide the blade in beside the key, turn it toward the key so its teeth sink into the key's soft brass, and then pull the blade out along with the key fragment.